STAGE DESIGN

STAGE DESIGN

TONY DAVIS

STAGECRAFT

RotoVision

A RotoVision Book
Published and Distributed
by RotoVision SA
Rue Du Bugnon 7
1299 Crans-Près-Céligny
Switzerland

RotoVision SA
Sales and Production Office
Sheridan House
112–116a Western Road
Hove, East Sussex, BN3 1DD, UK
Telephone: +44 (0)1273 72 72 68
Facsimile: +44 (0)1273 72 72 69
E-mail: sales@rotovision.com
Website: www.rotovision.com

10 9 8 7 6 5 4 3 2 1

ISBN 2-88046-506-0

Book designed by Lippa Pearce Design

Production and separations by
ProVision Pte. Ltd. in Singapore
Telephone: +65 334 7720
Facsimile: +65 334 7721

CONTENTS

"How can it be that in the theatre…in the West…everything that is **not contained in dialogue,** has been left in the background? I maintain that the stage is a **tangible, physical space** that needs to be filled and it ought to be allowed to be its own concrete language." Antonin Artaud

Antonin Artaud was one of many who raised complaints about how theatre is considered. Ever since Aristotle in his *Poetics* made drama an element of poetry, words have been dominant. Yet drama might have been part of choreography. Artaud contrasts the word-centredness of the Western performance tradition with the more even-handed Eastern tradition and encourages us to consider the overall achievement of performance, seeing it as "a kind of spatial poetry…confused with enchantment".

Stage Design examines the intelligence and creativity of those who illuminate performance with their intelligent spatial poetry. It brings together the striking achievements of 12 of the world's great stage designers gathered from five continents. As a text, the book consists of edited interview narratives in which the stage designers describe their ways of working. Over 50 productions from around the world are illustrated with sketches, models, plans, reference material, notes, storyboards and words. This book is a unique resource and is concerned to present stage design in a refreshing and sympathetic manner. The material is selected sometimes to show process, sometimes to help explain narrative sequence and sometimes because a stage design is so striking in its own right. All of the designers are mature artists who have produced a substantial body of work. Inside you will find a treasure chest of stage designs, including two breathtaking and contrasting designs for the four operas of Wagner's **Ring Cycle**, the spectacular designs for **The Lion King** and the evocative designs for **The Phantom of the Opera**. No one could have seen all of these operas, plays, musicals, dance performances and ballets. This book is not just about great stage designs, it's also about why and how these designs were created. It is for many kinds of reader including performing, visual and applied arts professionals and students, and for all live performance enthusiasts.

Design for the stage can be astonishing in itself or it can subtly modulate a production to reveal insights. Great design may draw attention to itself or it may have an unobtrusive presence. At its best, stage design answers many questions and poses others in order to create the imaginary space within which a production can occur. Stage design has always been a part of ritual and theatre and is always reinventing itself. It offers forms created by the mind within which performances can be played out. This is equally the case whether the stage is an empty space or whether it is filled with the machinery for **Les Miserables**.

The role of a dramatist, a librettist, a composer or a choreographer is fairly well understood. Even the role of a director is pretty much in the public domain. But the role and work of the stage designer is a mystery to most of us. In this book and in their own words, designers describe the process of design, what inspires them, how they work and what design means to them. Anyone who is looking for a text that offers a tidy and coherent account of design practice will be disappointed, not by this book but by stage design itself. These designers do not all know one another's work. None of them go about their work in quite the same way. Several hold strongly opposing views about design.

Stage Design offers an approach to creative practice. This means that the book does not offer conceptual unity or a progressive theoretical or developmental approach. Wildly varying creative artists have been corralled into this book; it barely contains them. That is the nature of creativity, for which we do not have an effective common language; neither do we understand how or why it occurs. This variety runs throughout the designers' work. At best it is possible to say that most designers sketch, that they usually create scale models and that they draw up plans to enable the scene shop to build their designs. Otherwise, diversity of approach is the rule. Some designers, such as William Dudley and Günther Schneider-Siemssen, articulate their developing practice with enthusiastic references to and engagement with technological advances. Ralph Koltai and Adrianne Lobel identify the importance of the moment when the design idea hits them; a moment that follows a lot of intellectual and practical work. Inspiration comes in many ways to each designer and may arrive in a different way for each show. As observers of the working methods of these artists, we are left in an interesting position: we cannot predict or measure inspiration and creativity; we don't have a language of value to apply to stage design and the designers don't go about things according to a formula. This is, of course, one of the reasons why this book is so interesting.

The term scenography was initially used in relation to the work of the legendary Czech designer, Josef Svoboda and intends to be an inclusive term that covers the impact and practice of the stage designer across a production. Yet Ming Cho Lee is one of those stage designers who offers a contrary view of the term: "We are really a kind of a ma and pa operation; it's very hands-on, very instinctive. The word scenographer almost involves too much: too much planning; too much painting; too much science; too much technology. I feel that we are people who create scenery; it can have a very modern or post-modern or contemporary look but, once the show is over, the set has no value. There's a temporariness about our work. It's just a little bit messier and less scientific, that's my bias against the word scenographer."

Almost all of the designers use technology of various kinds on stage but not all of them are as comfortable with using it to create their designs in the first place. Nor, for several reasons, do many stage designers have adequate archives of their work. Bill Dudley reveals an infectious enthusiasm for technology and was the only designer profiled who had a digital archive of his work: "I became an evangelist to other designers and I was met with a kind of hostile indifference. They were quite grumpy about it, saying that we would lose our individuality. I've never thought that and when I look at what I do with my computer, it is exactly my kind of handwriting. I don't use a mouse, I use a cordless pen and can suck the end of it without electrocuting myself. It's pressure sensitive so that, just like with the nib of a pen or with a pencil, I can emphasise and shade. Using it feels as though you are working on drawing pads or tracing paper. It's just that with the computer you can then collage-in pictures of your actors and use any kind of visual language like silhouettes, stamps or found objects. Also, it's sensationally good for creating the effect of light." These differences of opinion seem entirely healthy to me, especially as working conditions and cultural practices vary so much around the world. Whether it is called scenography or stage design, it was only during the later 20th century that it became widely available as an undergraduate course and as a discipline in its own right. Nor is it an easy career option for most. JC Serroni shoulders three major responsibilities: designing theatres in the mornings; running Brazil's first dedicated stage design school in the afternoons and also finding time to do his own scenography. As stage design evolves, many designers are pioneers and consciously pull others up the ladder after them. Some do this by employing assistants; others, such as Ming Cho Lee at Yale University, have overseen a whole new generation of designers.

For anyone reading this book for career guidance, the stage designers in this book tend to agree that a combination of study and apprenticeship offers the best preparation. Design requires a critically and historically informed, multidisciplinary intelligence as well as inspiration. And yet we lack the words adequately to discuss most kinds of design, including stage design. Despite this, stage designers have a remarkable plastic intelligence, an ability to relate form to ideas, to history and to narrative. During a period when each production of a play or an opera may look and feel quite different, design is clearly doing something original.

There have been many attempts to establish the status of design. During the 20th century in Europe, Edward Gordon Craig, Oskar Schlemmer, Antonin Artaud, Bertolt Brecht, Jiri Kroha, Roger Planchon and many others have wanted to see design established on a more equal footing with dramatic writing. In truth, stage design is still rather marginal and its achievements have been underestimated. Designers interpret and transform but they also create. The designers in this book are unified in claiming that their designs are not forced upon work and that they emerge out of collaboration. Yet designers are also sometimes vilified for creating a trivial theatre of spectacle. The media and the public are uncertain. It is evident that one of the reasons that people around the world flock to shows often has much to do with the design. Innovative design inspires people, just as it always has. Dominant stage design has been accused of arrogance and extravagance, notably in France during the 1980s. It holds true for collaborative art forms that, if any element becomes too overweaning, the whole effect can be spoiled. On the other hand, a design such as Ralph Koltai's for the musical **Metropolis**, can become the star of a show that is not itself successful. As words are often associated with sincerity and depth, so design is associated with ornamentation and surface – in this respect there is an inherent suspicion of design. These are false oppositions. The deeply textured,

historically informed approach of, for example, Bill Dudley alerts us to a critical design practice no less intelligent or sincere than the text of a work that he may be working on. When Ralph Koltai designs a concentration camp setting for Rolf Hochhuth's play **The Representative**, he is informed by his experience at the Nuremburg War Trials as well as by our common historical knowledge of that awful holocaust. This reveals an attitude toward stage design that is complex and demands our attention. The setting can be the imaginative and intelligent centre of a production.

In this book I wish to demonstrate that stage design has many virtues and strengths; the problem is that we are not visually literate. We revere what we are used to talking about. Judging by the relative difficulty of conducting international research for this book and the poverty of interesting materials about stage design that are easily available, this is a situation that can be changed for the better. Design is uncontainable and ever-changing. If we can find a way of relishing it, we can encourage it to flourish.

Most of these stage designers also design costumes but, apart from Jaroslav Malina's chapter, costumes have been largely overlooked in this book, mainly to allow room for the breadth of material showing design process. Much of this book is about design for theatres and opera houses but stage design is practised in many other settings too. *Stage Design* does not intend to create a premiere league of designers, only to present some outstanding aspects of global design practice. Many of the designers in this book have worked on film, television, exhibitions and other design areas. Adrianne Lobel, Yukio Horio, JC Serroni and Günther Schneider-Siemssen, for example, served significant apprenticeships in film and television. Many of the designers teach stage design and some of them direct productions. Some are artists by training and practice; others, like George Tsypin and JC Serroni, are trained architects. Each is different. All of them are first generation designers and all have a vibrant and pioneering spirit which I hope this book does something to capture.

I would like to thank all of the designers – Günther Schneider-Siemssen, Ralph Koltai, Ming Cho Lee, Guy-Claude François, Jaroslav Malina, Bill Dudley, Maria Björnson, JC Serroni, Yukio Horio, Richard Hudson, Adrianne Lobel and George Tsypin – for their generosity with their time, their ideas, their work, their archives and, in many cases, their writing; this is their book. In Oxford, the Bodleian Library and, in London, the British Library, the National Art Collections Library at the Victoria & Albert Museum, the Theatre Museum and the library at Wimbledon School of Art have all been helpful. At the Royal National Theatre in London, I would like to thank Bella Rodriguez, the Press Office and Louise Ray at the Archive. The translators, Ulrike Scholz, Lucia Pinto, Natsuko Tamura-Hammond, Alex Ward, Danièle Spiers and Lucy Brooks, have done a wonderful job. Also, thank you to our transcriber Judith Burns. Neil Wallace of Offshore Cultural Productions in Amsterdam was sympathetic and helpful. Lippa Pearce Design ably rose to the challenge of designing this attractive book. At RotoVision I owe thanks to my unflagging, instructive and enthusiastic editor Zara Emerson and to Luke Mitchell, Tina Bell and Rebecca Thorn, who all helped with the prolific research. Like stage design itself, this book is the result of a collaborative effort.

The greatest respect is owed to stage designers and design teachers around the world and to OISTAT which, together with the Society of British Theatre Designers and the other national scenographic organisations, performs an important advocacy and support role for stage designers. *Stage Design* is for Maddie, Joe and Sam and for my brother, Roger. It is dedicated to Simon McBurney and to Robin Whitmore, two inspirational artists who showed me the way.

" Only my ability for **imagery** and my **imagination** has enabled me to come up with something **new**. **"**

GÜNTHER SCHNEIDER-SIEMSSEN

Professor Günther Schneider-Siemssen studied in Munich and started his stage design career as an apprentice scene painter at the Bayerischer Staatsoper (Bavarian State Opera House). After working as a designer in theatre and film, he was appointed Chief Scenic Designer for the Landestheater in Salzburg, where he first used projections as scenery in 1952. In 1951 he began 40 years of work with puppetry for the Salzburg Marionettentheater (Salzburg Puppet Theatre) and it was there in 1985 that he pioneered stage holography. In Bremen between 1954 to 1961 he designed 90 productions, including the first of seven versions of Wagner's **Ring Cycle**. It was also during his time at Bremen that he began in 1958 to articulate his theory of the stage as a cosmic space, by designing, with the composer's encouragement, Hindemith's **Die Harmonie der Welt** (The Harmony of the World). His career extends from a groundbreaking production of Schoenberg's **Erwartung** at the Royal Opera House in London in 1957, through to Herbert von Karajan's invitation to work with him, which led to Schneider-Siemssen's long-term appointment as Chief of Scenic Design at the Wien Staatsoper (Vienna State Opera House). His career has embraced long-term relationships with several directors and with many theatres internationally. His interests include teaching at the International Summer Academy of Fine Arts in Salzburg and painting with light and projections, as well as researching the physics concerning holography and 3D lighting projection.

INTERVIEW: Originally I wanted to become a conductor. When I was ten years old, I saw a fairytale opera of **The Frog Prince** and loved the transformation scenes on the stage. That spirit of magic has stayed with me and is expressed in my stage practice.

My work is characterised by my versatility and adaptability; by my desire to make the content of a work visible to the public; by my use of technology and light to make scenes, and by making scene changes visible to the audience. I believe that a good stage designer needs imagination, flexibility, the ability to give a work an appropriate contemporary character and a familiarity with everything to do with the business of mounting theatre. The public will react positively, even for a modern piece, if the production works. There can be problems if a production is too preoccupied with itself and if it alienates the audience; if a staging is extreme but has ignored the meaning of the work; if money is squandered on materials that oppress the performers, and if the integrity of work is set in stone so that you cannot respond artistically to it.

A director may give stylistic ideas; otherwise there are three rules of play in my philosophy. The stage designer may have an idea that incorporates a concept for direction, which the director then animates; the director may have the original idea and this stimulates the stage designer. Or the director and designer work together to resolve an approach. For example, for the opera **Un Re in Ascolto** (The Listening King), the composer Luciano Berio provided no information about where the scenes were to be played and its content is difficult to recognise or see. The director Götz Friedrich and I had to think up the relevant scenes and places, which was a difficult task. I had no music score. As a basic concept we thought up a hydraulic lift, which could be adjusted to any height, with a cosmic, open circle for the main protagonists and choir. The various elements of the stage set were integrated into it. For example, the 3000 tears required were fabricated into the shape of droplets from plastic material and were lowered from above on thin wires. The audience could see the scene changes taking place. We tried to pin down a deeper meaning – quite the opposite from Wagner, Verdi or Mozart operas, where the librettists and composers provided precise information about what the scenery should be like and how it should be presented in the theatre. I found this to be a fascinating, exciting and imaginative task of a kind that the theatre can rarely provide.

I have always been known for my ability to create a cosmic experience on stage, and this kind of realisation has been aided through the improvement of technology over the years. When I designed the cosmic arena for **Die Frau ohne Schatten** (The Woman Without a Shadow) for director Herbert von Karajan in 1964 there were no technical innovations. The play was designed for the relatively small stage at the Vienna State Opera House. With difficult, brief interludes, the scene changes were carried out behind closed curtains.

UN RE IN ASCOLTO
By Luciano Berio
Salzburg Festpielhaus, Salzburg,
Austria, 1984
Directed by Götz Friedrich

1 Model: The scene for the second Duet and the third Aria
2 Production photo: The ship sails away
3 Model: The scene for the fourth Aria with falling tear drops

Schneider-Siemssen's sense of the cosmic, expressed in terms of projections, ellipses and the universe within which we find ourselves, realised itself in the world premiere of Luciano Berio's open-ended scenario, **Un Re in Ascolto** (The Listening King). An almost constructivist formalism to the design enables Schneider-Siemssen to locate the performers in a place which might be anywhere and which exists only for the duration of the opera, expressing his idea of the stage as a cosmic room. Tears fell and the ship sailed in the resulting sea of tears. Members of the chorus sang while hanging onto the open circle raised to an angle of 45 degrees. Children flew in the air. It was magical and mysterious yet executed with enormous precision. For Schneider-Siemssen this was one of his most significant achievements, especially given that he had to make something concrete out of an unspecified dream state.

1

3

2

1

Projections can create an image of cinematic expansiveness in
live performance. Schneider-Siemssen is able to create images
that are not just other-worldly but which can contain the whole
world or more on the stage; he is also able to generate a kind of
three-dimensionality with his projected images. This kind of
spectacle was initiated by Schneider-Siemssen in 1958 with a
visionary staging of Paul Hindemith's **Die Harmonie der Welt**
(The Harmony of the World) which combined projections, flowing
scenic elements that linked earth and the cosmos, and an elliptical
shape created by a large, convex cyclorama. In **De Temporum
Fine Comedia**, (The Play at the End of Time) Orff has created a
hugely ambitious opera, reminiscent of the vast scope of classical
Greek drama, of myths and of grand, philosophical, religious
narratives. With work like this the composers' requirements
defeat conventional approaches to staging and require a
massive imaginative input.

DE TEMPORUM FINE COMEDIA
By Carl Orff
Salzburg Festspielhaus, Salzburg,
Austria, 1973
Directed by August Everding

1 Production photo: Epilogue, The
new beginning after the Holocaust
2 Production photo: Epilogue,
Projection onto the iron curtain
3 Production photo: Act I, The
Sibyls and the tree of life
4 Production photo: Act II, The
Intellectuals sit before a telescope
and learn the truth from the stars
5 Production photo: Act II, The
Intellectuals escape in a dream
6 Production photo: Act III, The
last people
7 Production photo: Act III, The
last people. Fire appears in the
telescope

2

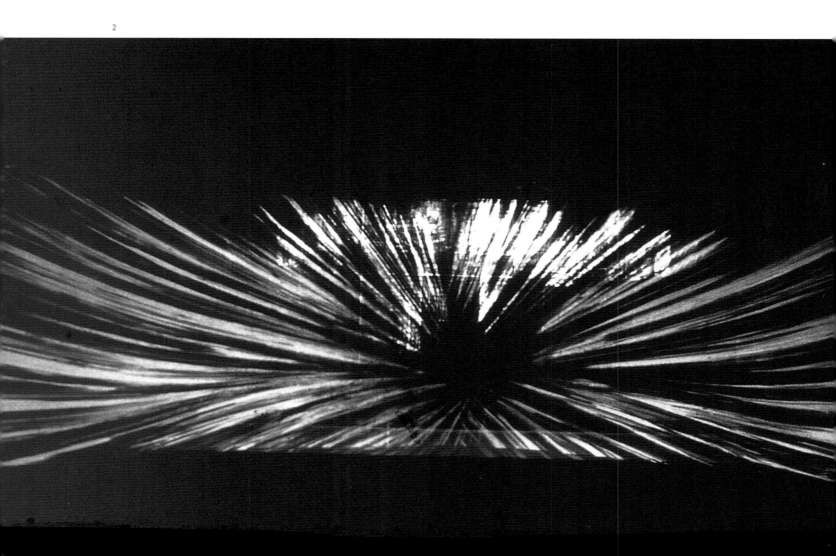

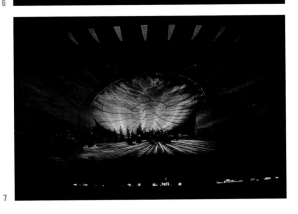

However, by 1974 lighting and projection technology had considerably developed and improved. When I designed **De Temporum Fine Comedia** (The Play at the End of Time) on the gigantic Salzburg stage, the scene changes were carried out under the gaze of the audience. Due to its great size, the Festspielhaus in Salzburg was ideal for producing Carl Orff's settings as a cosmic space that contains visions of light. Although the music profession asserts that the music for this opera is not strong, Carl Orff's subject matter is a testament to our humanity. The last humans? It is a disconcerting warning! I managed to draw the auditorium and the audience into this world of experience by using a transparent, rounded horizon made of tulle. This was particularly effective in combination with the simultaneous stage arrangement of the three worlds, (which we also showed in **Die Frau ohne Schatten** in 1964). The first world is that of the Emperor and the Empress, with the gardens floating over the second world, which is the earth-bound world of the dyer and his wife and, as the third dimension, the spiritual world, which intersects with and glides in and out of the two other worlds.

That production was one of my most challenging stage designs as I had to reveal a cosmic space and at the same time indicate the weightlessness of the theatre stage and the singers. When I am working with singers I use materials that are acoustically sympathetic. A raked stage needs to be able to offer support for the singers and their diaphragms. Performers need costumes that are light and comfortable. When I work with singers I show them my designs, explain the principles of the design and show them models; whereas the director will explain the directorial concept and the lighting design.

The first phase of my on-stage holography work began at the Salzburg Marionettentheater with the physicists Dr Kroy and Dr Halldorsson. The small holograms were projected, using argon lasers, onto glass surfaces covered with a foil holographic coating, where all the information was stored. The holograms were produced in England according to my designs. The second phase, intended for a large stage, such as the Bavarian State Opera House, never took place. The holographic laboratory in Los Angeles has the capacity to do it but the job could not be achieved in the time available. For this reason there needs to be a lot of time between awarding the contract to the date of the premiere. This is because during the research process there are bound to be failures and setbacks. We are now at the stage where we can physically implement holography on large stages. The main problem is the extremely high production costs. Now it is possible to make the holograms into three-dimensional images using special spots. We are currently working on laser projection with which it is possible to produce holographic images. There is huge potential for reducing the cost of touring performance once the technical challenges of holography can be overcome. However, currently holography is difficult to set up. My interest in this area and in high resolution projection on stage leads to seeing the lighting designer as an artist rather than as a technician.

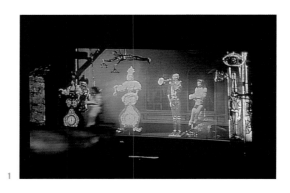

1

2   3

It is significant that Schneider-Siemssen should have worked
so long with the Salzburg Marionettentheater. As this world premiere of on-stage scenic holography makes clear, this tiny theatre
offered great technical opportunities. Puppet theatre is a rigorous
and imaginative form that is not always given the credit it should
be amongst theatre practitioners. Schneider-Siemssen has
predicted great possibilities for stage holography, from obvious
uses such as representing the devil in Goethe's **Faust** and the
witches in Shakespeare's **Macbeth** to many other visionary
opportunities. Here, in **Tales of Hoffmann** he was able to create
rooms and ghosts in broad daylight but, at that time, only green
or reddish-purple holograms could be projected. A hologram can
be animated on stage by being hit by a laser beam or a regular
light, enabling its deceiving form to be revealed to the audience.
We are still waiting for cost-effective holography for the stage.

5

6

TALES OF HOFFMANN
By Jacques Offenbach
Salzburg Marionettentheater,
Salzburg, Austria, 1985
Directed by Wolf Dieter Ludwig

1 Model: The Olympia Act,
revealing automated
holographic figures
2 Production photo: Act III,
Antonia at the piano
3 Production photo: Act III, Dr
Mirakel moves ghost-like
through the closed doors
4 Production photo: Act III, In
front of the real doors are
holographic doors, enabling
the ghostly effects
5 Model: Act II, Holographic
pillars and moving puppets
6 Model: Act II

I am well known for my productions of Wagner's **Ring Cycle**, having designed seven so far. Only my ability for imagery and my imagination have enabled me to come up with something new and to create and produce a different **Ring Cycle** each time. I rethink the four mighty operas on each occasion. My first production was in Bremen, Germany, and my second was in London at Covent Garden, with Solti and Hotter. I updated the basic concept from the Bremen production for London by creating a symbolic ring, thereby providing scenic and dramatic support into which all four works could be integrated. The ring could be changed to any height setting. The third **Ring Cycle** was with Karajan beginning in 1967 at the large Salzburg Festspielhaus. The Salzburg set was a cosmic ellipse divided into fragments that could be changed in isolation. All additional elements of the stage set were inserted compositionally into the ellipse. The fourth **Ring Cycle** was at the Metropolitan Opera House in New York from 1969 to 1971 and was based on the Salzburg production. And for the fifth **Ring Cycle** at the Teatro San Carlo in Naples I ensured that Wagner's cosmic thoughts were visible to the audience.

The sixth **Ring Cycle** with Jimmy Levine and Otto Schenk was a breakthrough. I moved away from the cosmos and created a renaissance of romanticism, a completely new Romanticism, in which, by means of lighting enhancements and innovative lighting technology, I created exciting imagery. My lighting design and the multiple use of projections were implemented in this production which was also a hit on video. Together with the lighting department, we constructed special new fire-effect equipment and were thus able to show the fire magician of the Valkyries. Then there was the seventh **Ring Cycle** at the Wielkitheater in Warsaw with August Everding and Robert Satanowski. It was very modern and still used my cosmic theme. A new eighth production has begun at the Wagner Festival 2000 in Wels in Austria with **The Valkyries**. This new concept shows the island of Iceland, the landscape of the mythological gods and original location of Richard Wagner's spiritual theme.

My advice to young designers is to learn the theory and the practice, the 'praxis', of theatre and stage design and to observe my Ten Commandments for the stage designer. Commandment One is that the stage should be developed as a cosmic or universal space. Two is that you need to study and achieve mastery in all aspects of theatre design. Three is that you must not kill the work. Four is that you should not be unfaithful to a good director. Five is that you must serve the work and actualise it on stage. Six is that you should be able to interpret music visually and, if you have no empathy for music, you should keep away from musical works! Seven is that, like a composer who has every instrument in his hearing, you must be familiar with and be able to deal with the whole technical operation of the stage, including lighting and special effects, so that something creative can develop. Eight is that you should avoid material struggles on the stage, like overspending the allotted budget, as this is to capitulate to your imagination and not to do your job properly. Nine is that you should make the universal and the cosmic visible to the public in projected light spaces. Ten is that, following Goethe, 'For the stage designer the actor, singer or dancer is the measure of all stage matters'.

2

RING CYCLE
By Richard Wagner
Royal Opera House, London,
UK, 1958
Directed by Solti and Hotter

1 Photograph: The construction of
the ring at full height (below)
2 Photograph: The ring being
pivoted to 45 degrees (below)

1

2

RING CYCLE: THE RHINEGOLD AND
THE VALKYRIES
By Richard Wagner
Metropolitan Opera, New York,
USA, 1990
Directed by Otto Schenk

1 Production still: The opening
scene of **The Rhinegold**. The
sun breaks through the water and
lights up the gold (previous page)
2 Production still: Act II, Siegfried
breaks Xotan's sword and shouts
to the Valkyries
3 Production still: **The Valkyries**,
appearance of Brunhilde, Death
and Annunciation
4 Production still: **The Valkyries**,
on the Valkyries rocks
5 Production still: **The Valkyries**,
The fire breaks out
6 Production still: **The Valkyries**,
the fire spreads

3

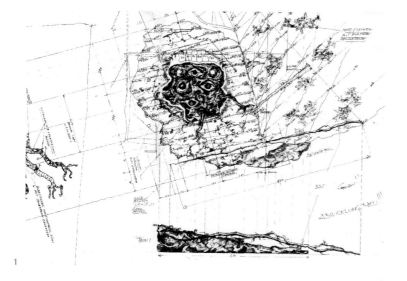

1

BLATT 4

2

The **Ring Cycle** by Wagner comprises four, interlinked epic operas: **The Rhinegold**, **The Valkyries**, **Siegfried** and **The Twilight of the Gods**. Schneider-Siemssen's eight **Ring Cycles** constitute a major achievement and can be usefully compared with George Tsypin's equally striking Amsterdam **Ring Cycle** (see pp157–159). Schneider-Siemssen comes into his own with this grand, Wagnerian vision of the need to renounce love for a greater good. The interplay of human emotions on a vast, mythic stage suits a sensibility that combines technological sophistication with a primal vision worthy of the painters Caspar David Friedrich and John Martin. For Schneider-Siemssen light is a medium of expression and offers three kinds of three-dimensional techniques: laser graphics, holographics and projection. The plan for the latest **Ring Cycle** for the Wagner Festival 2000 in Wels (1) reveals the depth of the back and front projections. Mounting two projectors side by side enables Gunther to approximate a three-dimensional image for the audience. This means that effects of stage depth can be created in order that fires and other atmospheric elements can be shown with an alarming sense of impact.

RING CYCLE: SIEGFRIED
By Richard Wagner
Wagner Festival, Wels,
Austria, 2000
Directed by Günther Schneider-Siemssen

1 Technical drawing: The stage from above for **Siegfried**
2 Technical drawing: The branches of the tree for **Siegfried**

4   5   6

" The play isn't about a door, it is about **somebody coming on stage"**

RALPH
KOLTAI

Ralph Koltai CBE came to England from Hungary when he was 13. A young woman he met in a London tea shop at the end of the war happened to be a ballet dancer and was the catalyst for him to pursue a career in stage design after his early, uncertain start with graphic art. He has won many awards, including the London Society of West End Theatres' 'Designer of the Year' and four Golden Troikas at the Prague Quadriennale. Internationally successful, with over 200 productions achieved over five decades, Ralph Koltai is still industrious and busy. Credited with introducing the idea of the 'theatrical concept' to English stage design during the 1960s, he has developed remarkable approaches to staging performance and, in many ways, has blazed a trail for the growing profession of scenography. Yet his concepts have always been grounded in integrity, sincerity and respect for the work. Events often interconnect for Ralph Koltai: he joined the army in 1944 and soon after the war found himself running the library for the British Prosecution at the Nuremberg Trials. In later life, he was to design Rolf Hochhuth's **The Representative**, a play that directly addressed the Holocaust. Designers, no less than other artists, may find that their lives can inform their art.

INTERVIEW: I came to Britain in 1939. I'd been in Berlin from 1933 to 1939 and it was not a good time to be there. I was brought over with the assistance of Quakers as a refugee and I worked on a farm in Scotland. How I became a designer was a complete accident. One day after the war I was having lunch with a friend in a small restaurant called Slaters in London, and there were two pretty girls sitting at another table and we started chatting them up. They turned out to be ballet dancers from the Sadlers Wells Ballet; one of them became my girlfriend. I had previously been studying graphic art but I wasn't really the right person for that subject so I thought, 'I have a girlfriend who is a ballet dancer, so why don't I do theatre design?' So I went to Central St Martins School of Art in London and applied for their course. I was accepted and that was the start of my career.

Whether I am designing or directing the most important way in is to find out what the play is about, the metaphor for the play, not where it takes place or whether the door is on the left or the right. The play isn't about a door, it is about somebody coming on stage. When in 1997 I put together my retrospective exhibition, I discovered to my astonishment that my concern with concept and with metaphor were there from the start, totally unconscious.

I have a reputation for not reading the text because it gets in the way of my ideas but this is because I work very instinctively and intuitively. There is a general belief that you have to study the text inside-out, read it twenty times. I have a problem reading the play through once! But it varies, of course, depending on the situation. I am currently working on a production of **Don Giovanni** and there are some very specific moments in Mozart's work and an awful lot of psychology, so I have to be a little bit more careful about what is happening in each scene.

You see, my talent is primarily to recognise the accident. Fifty years back, designers did drawings, and then models were made from the drawings. But you can't have an accident when drawing so I always work three-dimensionally now. It can happen when I put something in my model or knock something over which breaks, and I'll think it is much more interesting broken. The most notable accident I experienced was while planning the design for the musical **Metropolis**, based on the classic film by Fritz Lang. I had to create a machine room and wanted to make a setting of interlocking gears, a bit like the Chaplin movie *Modern Times*. I went to a car breaker's yard and bought a gearbox to take apart. Those gears didn't make a stage set for me but I had the two halves of the gearbox casing. I thought that on a scale of 1:25, that's the beginning of a machine room. Never mind the cogs. It was a highly complex and expensive production but I created a machine room based on that accident, seeing the casing by chance.

TAVERNER
By Sir Peter Maxwell Davies
Royal Opera House, London,
UK, 1972
Directed by Michael Geliot

1 Research material: 'Proportions
of the human figure', c1492, by
Leonardo da Vinci, Galleria dell'
Accademia, Venice, Italy
2 Model: Equality between
Monarchy and Church with the
jester at the centre
3 Model: The seesaw
4 Production photo: Act I
5 Production photo: Act II, The
jester spins the wheel of fortune
6 Production photo: Act II
7 Production photo: Act II

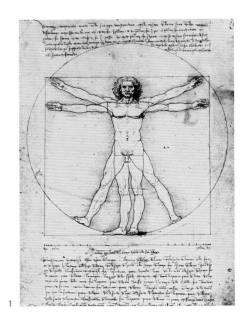

1

The 16th-century composer John Taverner had to weather the contradictions of being a great composer in the Catholic tradition, who then had to embrace Protestantism and consider separating himself from his greatest work: "**Taverner** is a good example of the need for a metaphor. It is about a confrontation between the Monarchy and the Church and the shifting of power, so I devised a set around a seesaw. Cardinal Wolsey was uppermost when the church was dominant during the Reformation in England; King Henry VIII was uppermost when his will prevailed." The seesaw was also used to represent the Renaissance conception of astrology and the wheel of fortune. The wheel at the centre of the stage would be spun by the jester to emphasise the randomness of the shifting of power (5). As the play developed Koltai increased the tension and dreamlike qualities through the use of small lights on the wheel of fortune and of pronounced garish colours on the background (6, 7).

Koltai found his inspiration for **The Planets** from older images of the planets as ever-circling spheres. Yet this metaphoric approach to representing the solar system was as much a technical as a conceptual marvel. There were mirrors on the sides and there was a two-way mirror at the back which was made from immensely strong polycarbonate, a material originally designed for use by riot police. To this a two-way mirror film could be applied. Small holes could be bored only a few centimetres from the edge of the 5mm- or 6mm-thick sheets in order to hang them. In Jupiter (3) the apple, a concept based on Magritte, is a painted flat hanging behind the mirror; it becomes visible, as with a gauze or scrim, when the mirror is lit from behind. The circular floor could tilt up and was manoeuvred by three hydraulic rams that could be linked up in various combinations.

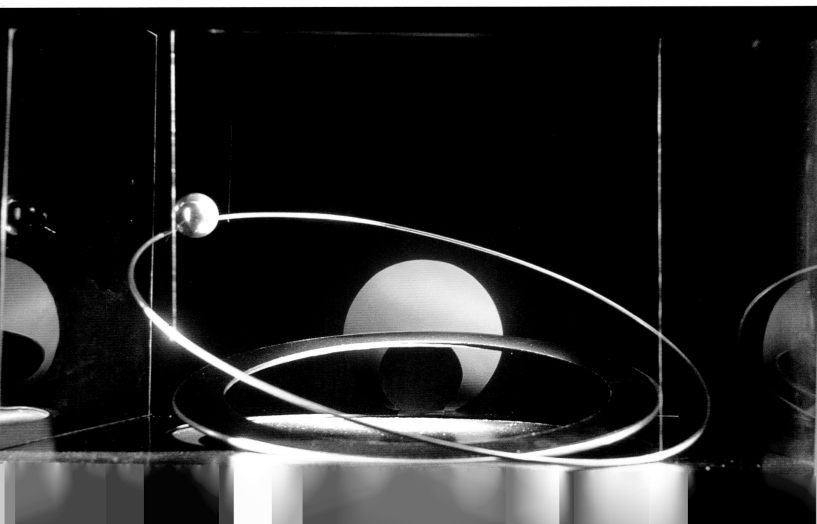

1

2

4

THE PLANETS
By Gustav Holst
Royal Opera House, London,
UK, 1990
Choreographed by David
Bintley

1 Model: Prologue, the earth
moves around the sun
2 Model: Mars
3 Model: Jupiter
4 Model: Saturn, the tilting
floor

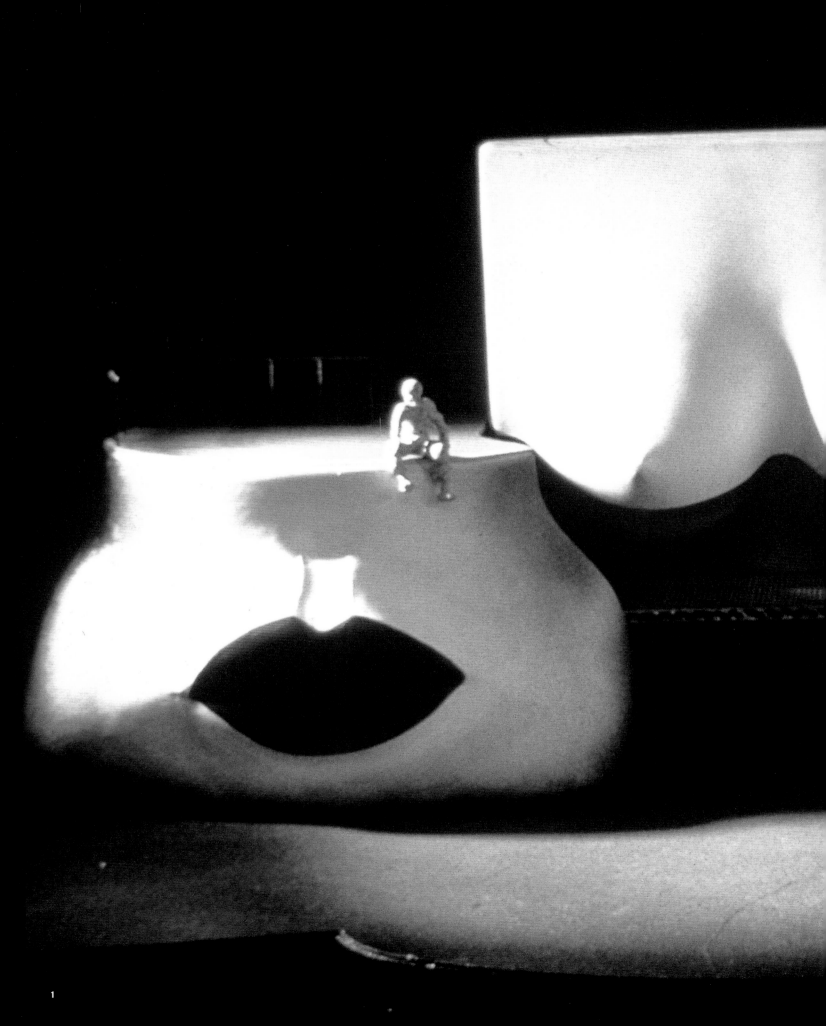

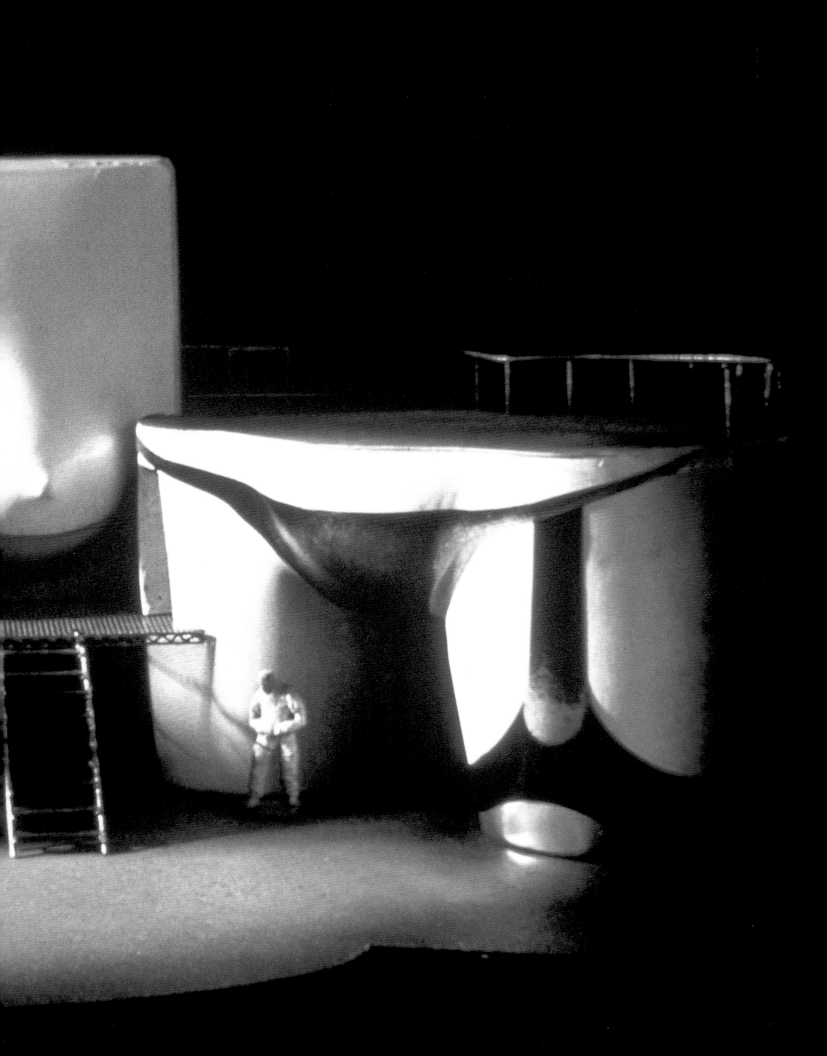

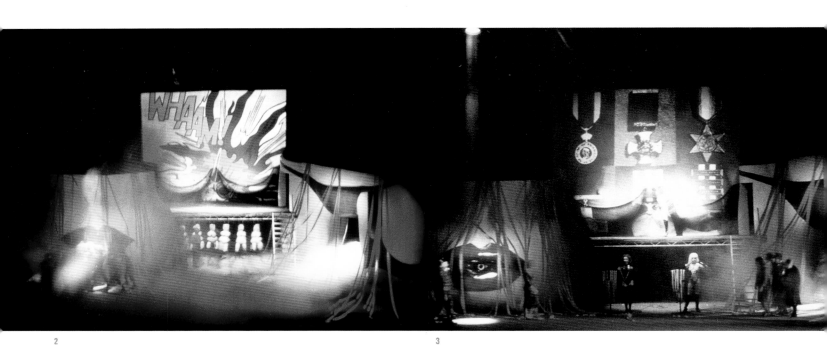

2

3

1

2

3

4

Zimmermann's **Die Soldaten** was designed for Ken Russell, whose straightforward request of Koltai was for an acting area with four levels. Reflecting the opera's critique of the degradation and abuse of women by the military in the 18th century, Koltai found his metaphoric solution by creating a three-dimensional, sculptural representation of a woman's body, fragmented into three white sections that could take a variety of projected images and lights. The dimensions of the Opera House in Lyons caused the biggest practical problem with this set: "The hall had a door only just big enough to allow a grand piano to pass through it. So the set had to be built in 46 pieces to allow it to get through the door and along the internal passageways; it was finally assembled on the concert platform."

DIE SOLDATEN
By Bernard Alois Zimmermann
Lyons Opera, France, 1983
Directed by Ken Russell

1 Model: The basic set (previous page)
2 Production photo: Final Act
3 Production photo: Final Act

Baal was produced on a tiny budget of £150 for the Royal Shakespeare Company's small studio theatre in Stratford. The theatre has no depth of stage, so in order to compensate, Koltai created a collage with three-dimensional props that could be placed and removed. Some of the structures like the bed could be pulled out from the wall to become part of a scene. The facade measured only 25x15ft and was no deeper than the width of the table. It was painted a pale, neutral beige so that it could take colour from lighting. At times the surface of the collage was taken over by projections. In this way the 20 scenes could be presented.

BAAL
By Berthold Brecht
Royal Shakespeare Company,
The Other Place, Stratford, UK,
1979
Directed by David Jones

1 Production photo: The basic set
2 Production photo: The convent
3 Production photo: The forest
4 Model: The basic set

On the other hand you can't design contemporary dance without observing the development of the choreography in rehearsals. You have to observe and live with the development; this in turn gives you a spark of something that you ought to create to make the production happen. In 1976 we presented a one-off dance piece, **Cruel Garden**, by Christopher Bruce with a scenario by Lindsey Kemp, at the Round House in London. The rather surreal scenario is based on the life of the writer Lorca. I thought, 'Lorca…Spain, I'll do a bullring'. This dance work turned out to be very successful and well received. I had to adapt it for conventional stages elsewhere. It has grown in stature and is still being re-mounted around the world. I can't remember now whether I developed the setting to match scenes in the piece or whether Bruce/Kemp created scenes because of the setting I had proposed.

Sometimes you get your solution from your materials. I have been using reflective materials in my design since quite early on in my life, ever since I designed an all-male production of **As You Like It** at the Old Vic Theatre with director Clifford Williams. Because they were all men, he originally wanted to stage the play in a sort of prison camp with towers on either side which had machine guns and search lights. I then suggested we set it in an Italian villa; a gay Italian aristocrat entertaining his friends. Clifford said to me, 'It's a very nice idea, but why are they doing **As You Like It**?' A fair question. So then, because of the style I had been working in, the reflective materials, I created a forest of Arden in a sort of abstracted way. The concept for staging it that way was the fact that all these people – Rosalind, Celia, Jacques – were having this romantic dream. It was a huge success and had an amazing cast. I remember Audrey was played by Anthony Hopkins. He absolutely hated having to wear a dress!

I think the nearest I've ever come to a definitive solution to doing a play was for Rolf Hochhuth's **The Representative** for the Royal Shakespeare Company. This play is about the Holocaust and criticises Pope Pius XII for his non-intervention. It wasn't really a question of design, it was the subject matter that was enormous. How do you put on stage the genocide of six million Jews? Where do you begin, so as not to trivialise it in some way? I had long discussions with the translator Robert David MacDonald and worried about it for weeks until one day it occurred to me that the metaphor for the play was a gas chamber. We had a false wall of concrete which closed off the proscenium at the front, onto which we projected documentary material of the period, sometimes accompanied by narration, while we did the half a dozen scene changes within the gas chamber box behind. That was what the play was about: a gas chamber and a memory.

The excitement of doing an opera tends often to be greater than the excitement of doing a play; there's something more majestic about an opera. But when an opera gets onto the stage, it frequently doesn't quite live up to that initial expectation because singers very rarely surprise you. I find that good actors will surprise you by coming up with amazing performances. Sir Peter Maxwell Davies' **Taverner** was an operatic exception. Benjamin Luxon, who played the dynamic

METROPOLIS
Adapted by Brookes and Hughes
from the 1926 film by Fritz Lang
Piccadilly Theatre, London,
UK, 1989
Directed by Jerome Savary

1 Research material: *Modern Times*, 1936, directed by Charlie Chaplin
2 Research material: *Metropolis*, 1926, directed by Fritz Lang
3 Model: The basic set showing the two halves of the gearbox
4 Model: Act I, The elevator which rises into the city above
5 Production photo: Act II, The rebellion by the workforce

role of the jester on the seesaw set, had previously been a physical training instructor. He volunteered to do things that you couldn't ask any singer to do and offered to jump off that 9ft-high centre platform onto the floor, do a somersault, stand up and sing. If an actor says that the set works for him and helps him to understand and perform the play, that is the biggest compliment I can receive. After finding the metaphor for the production, the second consideration is to make the actor feel he belongs to and is at ease within that space.

When working with other directors I find that the quality they are looking for in my design is a style that helps them to find a way of directing, of expressing the play. One thing that you need to be able to do as a designer, unless you are the sort of designer who is more like an interior decorator, is that you should be able to direct the play if you were called upon to do so. You have to say, 'Yes, I can do that play in that set'. When the director in me argues with the designer in me – if I realise that I will have a problem staging my design – then I find that the director always wins the argument.

Occasionally I have misjudged what the director wanted. I did Shakespeare's **Troilus and Cressida** with Howard Davies for the Royal Shakespeare Company. When I produced my design, he looked at it in total consternation. It was a very stylised image which focused on a different staging for each of the two opposing armies. Then I did a set that was inspired by the destruction of Tara in *Gone with the Wind*. I was not convinced that the differentiation between Greeks and Trojans was going to work in a permanent set. I had been sceptical; I had thought that Howard's vision of it was filmic but he made it work. That was an occasion where the director was really perplexed by what I had done originally. Despite a production being a collaborative effort, the designer is a very lonely animal.

What counts for me is the sense that it's important to produce a good piece of work, not just for the director and for me but for the whole organisation, the singers/actors, the technical team, the administration and, of course, the audience. I am quoted somewhere as saying that I give the director what he wants whether he knows it or not but it's true: you must remain honest to your own integrity. You cannot produce a piece of work and say 'Well, I don't like this much but that is what he wants'. The most important thing for a designer – and it can't really be taught – is to develop a pronounced critical faculty, because you are finally the judge. The other thing I always tell students is that ultimately you don't get employed for the quality of your work, you get employed because the director enjoys having coffee with you.

Technically, **Metropolis** was highly ambitious: "The two five-ton side sections that made up the machine room were so heavy that wheels could not be used for them; instead they were floated on air cushions, like a hovercraft. This meant that one or two people could move them as long as the sections rose a few millimetres from the floor." Koltai used three elevators to give the performers access to different levels: "When Maria leads the children to see the world of the elite class by using the centre-mid-stage elevator to the surface, there was a backdrop that evoked a metropolis like Manhattan (4). Behind the Manhattan panel, the green floor of grass was hanging vertically. When it was needed, it was lowered down the back wall and rolled forwards under the back-cloth across the floor. It had to be perfectly placed as there was only six centimetres' clearance for the elevator to come up through the grass. I used to watch that scene with my breath held."

"I prefer to **focus** on the **play** and the people in it and let the design **emerge** from the **life** of the play."

MING CHO
LEE

Ming Cho Lee arrived in America from China in 1949. He has led American design as a practitioner and teacher since the 1960s, establishing his vision most famously with a ground-breaking production of Sophocles' **Electra** for the New York Shakespeare Festival in 1964. Since then his work has involved a constant evolution from the past and a lively response to international influences. Lee progressed from the poetic realism that had been dominant in the USA since the 1940s and embraced new approaches to design. He attempted to discover the totality or core of a play and present this as emblem or icon in a formal space. His design tends to be presentational rather than representational in nature, sculptural rather than pictorial, existing in actual space rather than creating an illusionistic one. The extensive use of scaffolding gives the design a sense of the contemporary. He has also experimented with innovative materials such as beaten metal, occasionally with mixed media and with forms such as collage for the musical **Hair**.

INTERVIEW: It was mostly happenstance that got me into the theatre. I came from a business family that was deeply suspicious of the arts, with the sole but vital exception of my mother. I had always known that she was an amateur actress of some note but I recently discovered that she had far more involvement in the theatre than I knew. It was she who saw that I was trained – briefly – in Chinese landscape painting. And in Shanghai, between 1942 and 1946, she took me to see Western drama spoken in Chinese, as well as opera and some ballet. Later, at Occidental College in Los Angeles, I took a lot of studio art courses, especially watercolour and figure drawing, to balance my bad grades in anything language-related. These were a great preparation for set design. However, at that time, the American art world considered anything remotely representational to be 'illustration', a dirty word. Chinese painting, on the other hand, is never totally abstract; poetry and calligraphy are always part of the painting. So I have problems with totally non-objective abstraction; there is too much separation between visual symbols and words.

I decided I would never survive in the art world so instead I did all the sets for my small college and thought it was much easier than painting. Of course, the more I did, the harder it got. Had I gone to Yale then, when it was training designers for Broadway, I think I would probably know the history of decoration better than I do but I would not have been able to work for Martha Graham and probably would have had a much harder time doing Shakespeare. Instead, after a disappointing year at the University of California in Los Angeles, I became an unpaid apprentice and then junior assistant to Jo Mielziner, a major American designer. Jo was my mentor from 1954 until he died in the 1970s. In addition to Jo, between 1958 and 1961, I also assisted Boris Aronson. The two of them couldn't have been more different. While Jo was the quintessential theatre professional, Boris was a Russian-Jewish artist/philosopher. For Boris, designing for the theatre was not just a question of design but of the play's relationship to history, society, politics, religion – to life itself. His approach was often complex, ambiguous and very personal. I was also deeply affected by the work of Ben Shahn, a great political painter of the 1930s depression era. The epic theatre of Bertolt Brecht, never very popular in the US, entered my life at UCLA and became the foundation of my theatre thinking. And lastly, the seminal design of Isamu Noguchi for Martha Graham's dance theatre expanded the horizons of design for the stage. For a student of abstract painting, however unsuccessful I was, Noguchi was a true inspiration. The sculptural sets of the 1960s and early 1970s, especially at the New York Shakespeare Festival Delacorte Theater, were perhaps my attempt at bringing the theatre of Martha Graham to the legitimate stage.

Teaching and designing Shakespeare are the two most important experiences in my development. Teaching allows me to be in constant touch with the younger generation of theatre artists, to become immersed in their thoughts, their frustrations, their needs and their aspirations. It keeps me from isolation. As the principal designer for Joe Papp's New York Shakespeare Festival, I had the privilege of designing almost all of the plays in the Shakespeare canon, some

When he began working on **Khovanshchina**, Lee had become dissatisfied with the work he was doing and was becoming bored with the kind of emblematic, iconic approach to plays. The original design for **Khovanshchina** was highly realistic, closely resembling Russian landmarks; it was abandoned due to budget constraints and Lee's own lack of enthusiasm for it. Inspiration finally came to him while he was sitting at the stage door of the Mark Taper Forum in L.A., drawing on a stage door notepad and placing all the public scenes in a huge white box and all the interior scenes in a small confined space. The design was very radical for the Metropolitan Opera at that time and was not well received by New York critics but Lee felt it had moments of great visual impact: "It was my first attempt at postmodernism. The image was bolder, with less detail, and for me it was a significant step."

KHOVANSHCHINA
By Modest Mussorgsky
Metropolitan Opera, New York,
USA, 1985
Directed by August Everding

1 Model: Act I, Final 1:2 model
2 Sketch: Act III, Scene 1
3 Model: Act III, Scene 1
4 Sketch: Act I
5 Sketch: Act I
6 Model: Act I, Preliminary
1:8 model

1

2

3

4

5

6

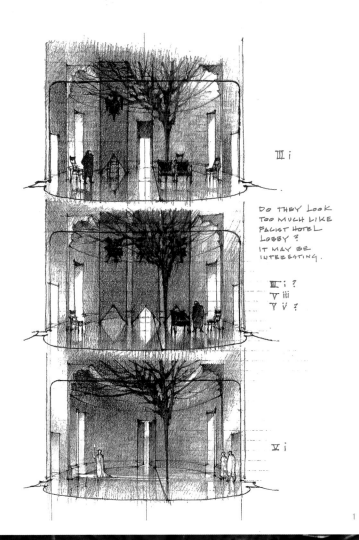

III i

DO THEY LOOK
TOO MUCH LIKE
FACIST HOTEL
LOBBY?
IT MAY BE
INTERESTING.

III i ?
V iii
V v ?

V i

Lee sought to create a production of **Macbeth** that was truly frightening: "I felt that **Macbeth** required serious examination in order to get to the darkest side of this play – an evil that is layered and not immediately visible." He initially sought to create a world which was pristine, clean and neoclassical where everything had the appearance of being correct and right. His notes from one of his storyboards (1) reflect his thoughts about it going too far in resembling a Nazi hotel lobby. He decided to make the three witches look like the sisters in Chekhov's **Three Sisters**, sitting in white rocking chairs in the middle of the heath. While some of these ideas were adopted, Lee felt that the concept was never really considered as a whole and the choices were rather arbitrary: "Why was this red tree sitting in this big red-splattered room? Who were the three witches? I don't think we answered these questions. It was very striking and well received but it never got beyond the usual **Macbeth** look, and I was never truly frightened."

3

MACBETH
By William Shakespeare
Shakespeare Theater,
Washington D.C., USA, 1995
Directed by Joe Dowling

1 Storyboard: Various scenes
for Act IV
2 Production photo: The
coronation for Act IV
3 Production photo: The
basic set
4 Sketches: Costumes ideas
and comments on the character
of Duncan
5 Storyboard: Various scenes
for Act IV

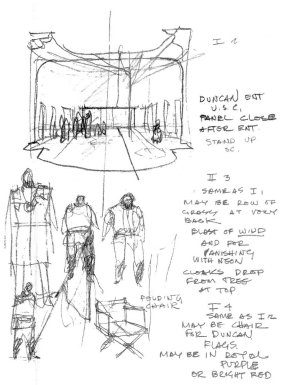

I 2

DUNCAN ENT
U.S.C.
PANEL CLOSE
AFTER ENT.
STAND UP
SC.

II 3
SAME AS I 1
MAY BE ROW OF
GROSS AT VERY
BACK
BLAST OF WIND
AND FOR
VANISHING
WITH NEON
CLOAKS DROP
FROM TREE
AT TOP

II 4
SAME AS I 2
MAY BE CHAIR
FOR DUNCAN.
FLAGS.
MAY BE IN ROYAL
PURPLE
OR BRIGHT RED

FOLDING
CHAIR

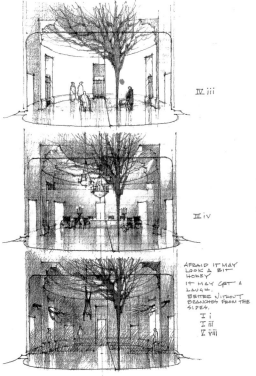

IV iii

III iv

AFRAID IT MAY
LOOK A BIT
HOKEY
IT MAY GET A
LAUGH.
BETTER WITHOUT
BRANCHES FROM THE
SIDES.
I i
I iii
IV viii

4

5

more than once. What an education! What a way to grow and mature! Today I cannot imagine a life without Shakespeare.

The late Garland Wright once said that theatre is an act of transformation. Actors transform words into living people engaged in human events and designers transform words into pictures, visual imagery, the physical world within which the events take place. Though not the originators of the work of theatre, we are more than mere interpreters. Our role demands a creative process that is often daunting but always rewarding.

I don't design with a specific audience in mind. I design for my collaborators and ultimately for myself. I have to assume that the audience is as intelligent or as stupid as I am, that it sees things the way I do. It is a form of arrogance to design or direct for an assumed, lowest-common-denominator audience. It implies that we know more than they do and that is inexcusable.

My design process and the way I collaborate with directors have both changed since the 1960s, due in large part to the inclusion of students of directing in my first year class at Yale. I discovered that, in order to work meaningfully with directors, the designer must think as a director, rather than force the director to think as a designer. Until the mid-1970s I tended to deal with a play mostly in visual terms and forced the director to do the same. This approach, especially for Shakespeare at the Delacorte Theater, resulted in sets that were relentlessly iconic and now seem formulaic, generalised and lacking a sense of emotional involvement. Today I prefer to focus on the play and the people in it, and let the design emerge from the life of the play.

I have also learned not to expect to arrive at a design in a single, continuous step. Now, if I have a problem grabbing hold of the core of the play or find the characters remote, I may start by designing what the playwright has written about the environment – often quite realistically – and through that process discover his or her intent. Occasionally I start by placing the play in a contemporary setting, just to give it a more immediate context. That exercise seems to liberate me and provides a basis to try something unexpected, unreasonable or dangerous. Lately I find exploring different options to be the most exciting part of the design process.

After doing the appropriate research – including looking at past designs and recent productions from England – and after the first meeting with the director, I start doing rough sketches, generally in 1:8 scale, on very cheap paper – legal pads. They are essentially a storyboard rather than drawings of scenery. When these seem to have some merit or when the response to them seems positive, I start a 1:8 model. At this point I prefer 1:8 to anything larger, since it allows me an overall view of the design without being distracted by details. You can cheat a lot and they are easier to build. I usually draft everything out to the point that my assistant can build the model and we often have several versions. When a choice

MING CHO LEE

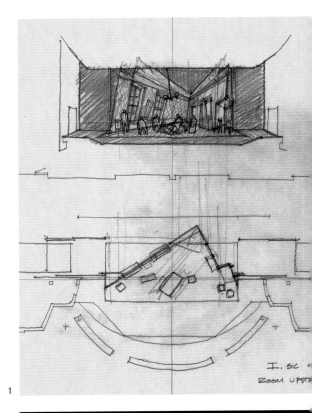

1

2

THE HOLLOW LANDS
By Howard Korder
South Coast Repertory Theater,
Costa Mesa, California, USA, 2000
Directed by David Chambers

1 Sketch: Hotel Room scene
2 Model: Hotel Room scene
3 Model: Inscription Rock scene
4 Model: Cult scene
5 Model: Missouri River scene
6 Model: Salt Flats scene
7 Reference material: Influence for Cult scene
8 Sketch: Early rendering for Back Yard scene
9 Model: Back Yard scene
10 Production photo: Hotel Room scene (overleaf)

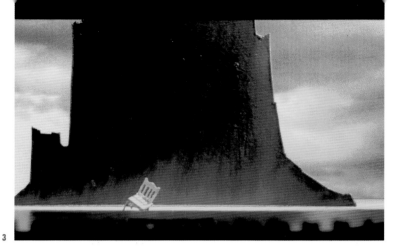

3

4

5

6

Lee found **The Hollow Lands** an inspiring play, one "that actually deals with a page of history". Throughout the 20th century, cinema has often co-opted the epic canvas. In the USA, movies set in the pioneering West at and after the time of **The Hollow Lands**, helped to create the popular idea of American enterprise and character. Lee had to find a way of creating an effective and distinctive design for this episodic story with its shifting locales and its scenic variety. His design had to hold its own in relation to iconic, cinematic visions of the American past. Lee created a haunting, theatrical vision of America's 19th century that complements our memory of Western movies and visual arts, just as Richard Hudson's designs for **Oklahoma!** create a uniquely theatrical version of Americana (see pp126, 128).

7

8

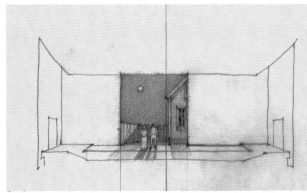

9

Rashomon was the first opera Lin Hwai-Min directed. With permission from the opera house, Lee created a ramp, a hanamichi in the Kabuki tradition, in the centre aisle so that characters could make long entrances through the audience. "I thought it would be interesting to have a mirror image of the auditorium on stage and to have a long entrance coming from upstage. When the singers came from the audience, doubles came from the back of the stage. The judge sat on the balcony on stage; another judge sat in the real balcony in the auditorium. While the characters in the opera were in period Japanese costume, the jury – the chorus – were all in black suits and white face make-up."

RASHOMON
By Miyako Kubo
Grazer Opernhaus, Graz, Austria,
1996
Directed by Lin Hwai-Min

1 Photograph: The opera house in Graz, on which the set was based
2 Model: The basic set
3 Production photo: The basic set

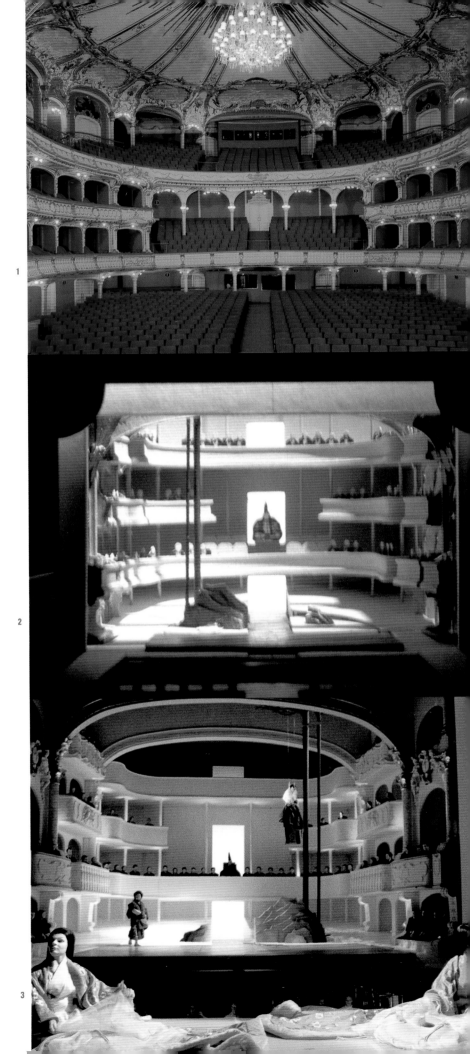

is finally made from the 1:8 model, we start a 1:4 model. I haven't done a finished sketch or rendering since designing Bellini's opera **i Puritani** in 1975 and even that was an exception. Two-dimensional painting is simply not a viable step for designs that are essentially three-dimensional and spatial in nature. It is a waste of time for me.

The design I have chosen as the anchor for this chapter is a recent production of **The Hollow Lands**, by Howard Korder, for the South Coast Repertory Theater. Unlike many current American plays – intimate, psychologically-based family dramas, **The Hollow Lands** is a play of extraordinary scope. It follows a young, Irish immigrant from his arrival in 1815 to 1859; it moves from New York, across the country, to the salt flats of Utah. Along the way it examines the people who made those journeys and the ways the country changed. A tough, unsentimental, violent and yet strangely moving play with 15 sets, it is bigger than the stage of the South Coast Rep could accommodate. David and I decided to design the play as written, giving each scene its full value. I did a full storyboard, a 1:8 model and a 1:4 model, eventually reducing the design to a barely manageable size.

I still feel that there must be a simpler way of doing this mammoth show, perhaps as Graham Vick and Paul Brown reduced Shostakovitch's opera **Lady Macbeth of Mtsensk** to a single setting for the Metropolitan Opera House. However, all of our attempts seemed arbitrary and forced and we never got there. Perhaps the lack of a single setting or of an overriding unity is what the play is about. I must admit, however, that the design was often quite exciting. It was very eclectic as expressionism coexists with endless surreal space, with the addition of occasional, strong, arbitrary colour. I felt I had entered uncharted territory.

The life of a theatre designer in the States is not an easy one, especially for someone like me who has had a less than distinguished career in the commercial theatre. However, in retrospect, I have few regrets about my choice of profession. For me, theatre is an arena where one wrestles with the issues of life. Theatre at its best challenges one's preconceptions, one's intellect, and expands one's capacity to feel. Through theatre one discovers one's self. This is why I have real problems with theatre of spectacle for its own sake. It is dehumanising and a cynical form of escape – the antipathy of what I consider theatre should be. Designing for theatre is a life-work. It is only possible for me when my work is informed by my life experience and when my life is enriched by my work. This is unique to the arts. Few other professions can make such a claim.

1

"There are designs where I feel I have reached a certain point of development, but that doesn't mean that I have done definitive work. There is no question that the 1964 **Electra** was both a starting point and a landmark. I think it affected the nature of American design. Would I do it that way now? I hope not."

ELECTRA
By Sophocles
New York Shakespeare Festival
Delacorte Theatre, New York,
USA, 1964
Directed by Gerald Freedman

1 Model: The basic set

"Scenographers create a **metamorphosis;** their **sensory intelligence** and design practice emerge from " studying the text.

GUY-CLAUDE FRANÇOIS

After studying at the Louvre School and at the National School of Theatre Arts and Techniques Guy-Claude François soon joined up with Théâtre du Soleil, working with Ariane Mnouchkine as technical and scenographic director in the reclaimed industrial setting of the Cartoucherie, an old armaments factory in Paris. This famous collaboration has continued for more than 30 years and has included **Tambours Sur la Digue** (Drums on the Dam) (2000) by Hélène Cixous. François's versatile career embraces many kinds of work: collaborations with architects to make and conduct feasibility studies for theatres; art direction and production design for films with directors such as Bertrand Tavernier, Philip Kaufman and James Ivory; international theatre and opera production; scenography for groups like the Vietnamese Water Puppets, exhibitions of his work, and exhibition and special event design, including the opening and closing ceremonies of the Winter Olympic Games held at Albertville, France in 1992. Since that year he has also been co-ordinator of the Scenographic Department at the Higher National School of Decorative Arts in Paris. He is the co-founder of the organisation 'Scene', which develops the scenographic aspects of architecture and vice versa. François has won many awards for his design for the stage and for films.

INTERVIEW: I believe in the unity of scenographic work, whether for films or for the stage. Scenography is a practice with a great range. This unity – a unity I teach my design students – depends upon the text as the source and content of the work. Before any notions of direction or design, there is a text. This text is the point of departure, the anchor and the brief for our work. Our agenda is determined by words, by thoughts and by poetry, all brought together in the stage designer's practice. The first responsibility of the scenographer is to love reading and to be able to read with wisdom. It is important to love working with texts and to try to understand and to interpret them before attempting to make a transformation between what is read, what is said and what finally is seen on stage. Scenographers create a metamorphosis; their sensory intelligence and design practice emerge from studying the text. Most of my ideas come from reading the text and even more so from what I read between the lines. That said, some directors inspire me, not by telling me the settings they like but by convincing me that their vision of the text is appropriate.

I think that theatre is a collective art, where everyone works off each other's skills. The director is, in the best cases, the interpreter of a text, the manager of everyone's skills and the co-ordinator of the whole show. I said, 'In the best cases' because many directors wait for the designer's first sketches in order to start their work. I think that stage designers should be regarded as highly as composers. In France, they are regarded as the creative artists who conceive the structure of a show, just as composers conceive the musical parts.

In general and especially when I don't know the director with whom I'm working, I do some sketches from the text that I've been given. I read the text alone and then make a design proposal in the form of a sketch that interprets what I have read. The discussion takes off from this sketch for two reasons. First, it's in making this transposition from the text that I learn to understand the text better, what's in the lines and between the lines – or, more exactly, with my sketch, I find out what I understood and made of the text! Secondly, it's the mutual understanding that you have of a text that becomes the yardstick for the relationship you'll have with the director. The complicity you have should be experienced as a free and equal relationship. Also, it is better not to distort the initial reading with any bias or presumptions about the text.

It's on the basis of these initial sketches of mine that the director and I come to our agreement. They serve, in some way, as a means of working out how we can conspire together to do the show and how our working relationship is likely to develop. I abandoned one production after a major disagreement that quickly became apparent, thanks to this way of working. Generally I prefer to work

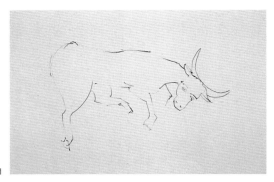

1

2

3

L'Indiade was a play about the history of the partition of India and Pakistan and about the history of India's independence. The brief was to create a sense of the place and the period for the audience and the actors. "The building materials that were most important to me were clay and marble; most of the décor was made with real clay and marble. The game between the marble, which is a material of great nobility, and clay, which is a poor material, played very well in this design; it spoke like a metaphor for India. More than that, the lighting on the marble created reflections a little bit like water, which you see a lot of in India."

L'INDIADE
By Hélène Cixous
Théâtre du Soleil, La Cartoucherie,
Paris, France, 1987
Directed by Ariane Mnouchkine

1 Drawing: The sacred cow
2 Set photo: The clay bricks
3 Set photo: The basic set

L'AGE D'OR
Collectively devised by the company
Théâtre du Soleil, La Cartoucherie, Paris, France, 1975
Directed by Ariane Mnouchkine

1 Set photo: Guy-Claude François works the bulldozer
2 Production photo: The audience enters
3 Set photo: The raked, carpeted floor and the illuminated ceiling

L' Age d'Or (The Golden Age) was François' first collaboration with Ariane Mnouchkine in the huge space of the Cartoucherie: "It was very evocative. What's interesting about the process is that Ariane wanted me to create a 'utopian space'. For me a utopian space is a space without reference to anything else. I made a model, a box with sand in it; and with my hand I sculpted some spaces for the actors and the audience." Mnouchkine and François decided on a final form which was four circular holes, at the end of which the actors acted and on the side of which the spectators sat; these areas were like small hills. Between each of the scenes, the spectators and the actors changed circles. The hills and holes were covered with brushed carpet. "I found that the best way to make the foundations was to sculpt with my hands in the model box. Then I learnt how to drive a bulldozer so I could do the same thing in the Cartoucherie."

1

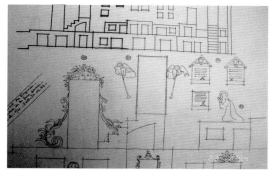

3

2

4

La Ville Parjure (The Treacherous Village) took place in a universal city of death, a cemetery. The difficulty for François wasn't to conceive an architectural invention but to create an authentic sense and feel of a cemetery without invoking any religion. Its scale reveals the ambitious nature of François' work with Théâtre du Soleil and how the engaged and politically committed stance of the company led to a sense of spectacle accompanied by great integrity.

LA VILLE PARJURE
By Hélène Cixous
Théâtre du Soleil, La Cartoucherie, Paris, France, 1994
Directed by Ariane Mnouchkine

1 Sketch: The basic set
2 Sketch: The basic set
3 Set photo: The basic set
4 Set photo: The basic set

2

For **Les Atrides** (The Family of Atreus) François adopted an archaeological approach to recover a sense of the mythic. A pit was hollowed out, reflecting the way that the play had unearthed the story. The scenography also refers to the fall of the Chinese Emperor Qun, who was locked up in his tomb with thousands of pottery soldiers.

LES ATRIDES
By Aeschylus and Euripides, adapted by Ariane Mnouchkine
Théâtre du Soleil, La Cartoucherie, Paris, France, 1990
Directed by Ariane Mnouchkine

1 Set photo: The pottery soldiers
2 Sketch: The basic set

with a director and with other contributors with whom the exchange of ideas is of such high quality that we can move on quickly from the text to our approach to the production. I think that to click with the director – who's a kind of partner in crime – is very important. And for those collaborators that I don't know, I do sketches and drawings, from the first day that we meet each other, in order to instil the partnership between us.

I work by hand but, for more technical drawings, I or someone else does them on a computer. In the theatre, digital technology is only a tool, it doesn't replace the designer's vision. A stage designer needs to be able to do everything. There are those who are technical virtuosos with digital imaging but often that is all they can do. You can't go 100 per cent digital in the theatre, if only because you can't sit on digital chairs or drink a digitally-generated drink. You need to be familiar with new technologies but also to know when it's most appropriate to use them.

I have assistants who have been friends for a long time; they are good critics and help me to understand what I do. After listening to them, I can explain scenography better to other people. When I teach I really focus on the creative aspects of my students, I teach them how to be creative as opposed to imposing my ideas on them. Teaching is a rich experience and has made me address the question: 'What are the roots of our profession?'.

By chance I travelled a lot when I was very young which has helped me in my work. I think being adaptable, having an interest in set design and its forms of expression – such as design and structural arts – are great assets. My training included classical studies and the history of art; I went to a design academy and studied stage design at theatre school. To become a set designer you must be able to read, draw and build. You need to be interested in many areas, to be cultured and to be audacious. It's a mistake to think that you can create scenographers who are masters of their art during a two-year course. I think that scenographers have to see deeply into whatever they are dealing with and to find imaginative ways of creating stage designs. Scenographers also need to know the operational side, how to work correctly, for example, with wire and other materials.

I think that in France, as in other European countries like Great Britain, we don't characterise 'typical' style any longer because the thing about our country now is hybridity, the combination of styles and forms. I find it increasingly interesting that this mixture becomes richer and richer; you can hear it most obviously in music; you can also see it in design. I don't think there's a particular French 'style' any more. A lot of people say to me you must retain a French style but I think they're wrong. It's much better that there isn't a French style. You could perhaps talk about a European style but I don't think that's right either as the influences are global. I think what's interesting is the permeability of the different arts. In France our art is comprised of very different arts, including those from Algeria.

The idea for **Macbeth** came to François when he saw on a map the forest in which the real Macbeth had battled with the English, before returning to his castle: "At the time this forest was huge, like many forests in Europe, and I imagined that it was terribly frightening, and that the trees had branches, like arms or like serpents, which imprisoned people."

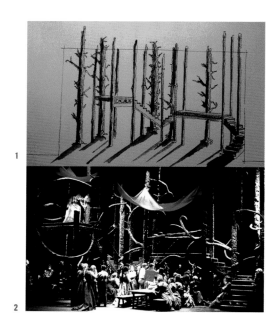

1

2

MACBETH
By Guiseppe Verdi
Opéra de Nancy, Nancy,
France, 1994
Directed by C. Mast

1 Drawing: The forest
2 Production photo: Act IV

Ariane Mnouchkine wanted to present three Shakespeare plays
– **Richard II**, **A Midsummer Night's Dream** and **Henry IV** – on
the same stage. The difference between the productions was in
the costumes and in great rolls of silk at the back of the stage.
Mnouchkine wanted to present the shows using South-East Asian
forms of theatre, in particular Japanese Kabuki and Noh Theatre:
"She thought that the strength at the heart of Japanese theatre
was ideal for expressing the situation of Richard II. Ariane adopted
my proposal to use silk. The advantage of the big curtains was
that, as the show went on, they descended little by little. It was a
metaphor for the theme of 'separation' but, above all, to mark the
passing of time."

RICHARD II
By William Shakespeare
Théâtre du Soleil, La
Cartoucherie, Paris, France, 1981
Directed by Ariane Mnouchkine

1 Production photo: Act I
2 Production photo: Act IV

A MIDSUMMER NIGHT'S DREAM
By William Shakespeare
Théâtre du Soleil, La
Cartoucherie, Paris, France, 1981
Directed by Ariane Mnouchkine

3 Painting: Exploration with colour
and form
4 Production photo: Act II

In **Life is a Dream** the throne room was very big and the shadows changed according to the scene. François achieved this effect with 'découpage', a cut-out from black fabric: "The problem that I had was that I made the model with a watercolour. The best way to reconstitute this way of making it was to use fabric with projectors so that the focal point could be changed. That allowed me to obtain the blurred parts on the sides."

LIFE IS A DREAM
By Pedró Calderon de la Barca,
Théâtre de Vasteras, Stockholm,
Sweden, 1992
Directed by O. Krejca

1 Set photo: Showing the découpage effect

1

THE MISER
By Molière,
Théâtre de Vasteras, Stockholm,
Sweden, 1992
Directed by O. Krejca

1 Set photo: The paranoid faces

For **The Miser** François wanted to find a way of linking the audience and the actor in this classical theatre: "A large cloth covered the stage and the auditorium. The faces were painted so that they were all looking at the actors who were placed in a very precise position on the stage. This accentuated the paranoid aspects of their characters."

THE MISANTHROPE
By Molière
Atelier Theâtral, Brussels,
Belgium, 1989
Directed by A. Delcampe

1 Production photo: Act II

The set for **The Misanthrope** was constructed in Plexiglass to
emphasise the 'transparency' of Celimene's house, which was
open to everyone. The theory was that the décor would transform
fibre-optically with light, which circulated throughout the interior of
the décor. The design was intended to convey the spirit of political
Realism in Paris after the Second World War. François put in place
several systems of special effects, optical and mechanical, to allow
the audience to apparently see the actors going through the
walls on stage.

TERRE ÉTRANGÈRE
By Arthur Schnitzler
National Theatre of Finland,
Helsinki, Finland, 1990
Directed by O. Krejca

1 Production photo: Act II
2 Painting: Explorations for
the rose theme

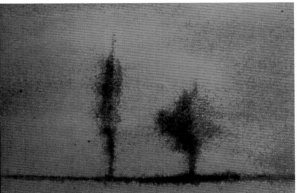

The set for **Terre Étrangère** (Undiscovered Country) represented
a huge field of roses. François researched plants for this production
because the play takes place in a house. "I found it interesting
to show a manicured garden because the story of the
Terre Étrangère is about the idea of being tamed."

1

2

Mephisto is the story of a German actor in the 1930s who left his committed theatre troupe for the official theatre, which was run by the Nazi government. Mnouchkine's adaptation was clear-cut and extremely provocative. There were two theatres. The audience were sat on swivelling chairs in front of the official theatre but behind their backs was the other theatre: "During the show we could change theatres. We not only changed the theatre the audience was looking at; we completely changed the architecture of the space. The Théâtre du Soleil is known for that, for totally transforming the space."

MEPHISTO
By Thomas Mann, adapted by
Roman Duclos Mann and
Ariane Mnouchkine
Théâtre du Soleil, La
Cartoucherie, Paris, France, 1979
Directed by Ariane Mnouchkine

1 Set photo: The 'unofficial
theatre'
2 Set photo: The 'official theatre'

1

2

For his two films, *Molière* and *Jefferson in Paris* François was able to create film sets that included an 18th-century theatre. At that time theatres were always catching fire; they weren't built from hard materials but were built like theatre sets: "It amused me that the artifice of film set construction was in a way authentic."

MOLIÈRE
Written and directed by Ariane
Mnouchkine, 1978

1 Production still: A travelling
theatre (above)

JEFFERSON IN PARIS
By Ruth Prawer, 1993
Directed by James Ivory

2 Production still: A travelling
theatre (above)

We use the term 'scenographer' more widely than 'stage designer' in France. For me, in the industry, it's a term that represents the fundamentals of what I do. I'm not just creating in a sub-contracted way the stage design or, say, the masks for a show; my work is more about the structure of the story itself. Architecture is the art of construction and I think architecture naturally is part of the field of interest of scenography. Of course, you could equally say that scenography is architecture. Above all, I always try to be fair. I don't attempt to create anything beautiful. I just ask myself if I'm doing justice to the text, to the director's concept and to the work of the actors. If a set is to be beautiful, it will emerge organically as beautiful but as a consequence of addressing issues in the text. This means I'm very versatile but, in spite of this, many people recognise the settings I do.

The costumes and the lighting are important in this tightly-knit work. If one small piece of a show is wrong, the whole thing is affected. In general, I try to work with the same costume and lighting designers. With regards to actors, I like to know them, to know if they're physical, if they are informed by culture, if they are like friends. Many actors tell me that they like acting in my settings.

Conceptually there's little difference for me between working for film or for the theatre. Both media are interested in the significance of the spaces and the objects, how to make them work for the audience. The main difference is in the techniques used. In the theatre there's a great tendency to design by using metaphors to communicate an idea or a situation. Film directors like to work with stage designers not only because of their ability to get to the essence of a text but also precisely because of their ability to come up with the right metaphor. You see, I think that film realism is also metaphorical. An object in a film can be symbolic of an action or of a situation. A field of wheat in which there is a lone chair is a metaphor for solitude, for example.

I am not concerned with posterity nor am I sentimental about my scenography; I greatly enjoy destroying my work when a show is over. It's more important to me that people know me as a multi-faceted designer. Many theatre people are unaware that I do sets for cinema, opera, architecture, education, puppets and museums. All of these are only facets and I cannot break up my work. However, despite all the work that I have done, I have a preference for the work I've done with Ariane Mnouchkine and Théâtre du Soleil, in particular **L'Age d'Or** (The Golden Age), the film *Molière*, the three Shakespeares and **La Ville Parjure** (The Treacherous Village).

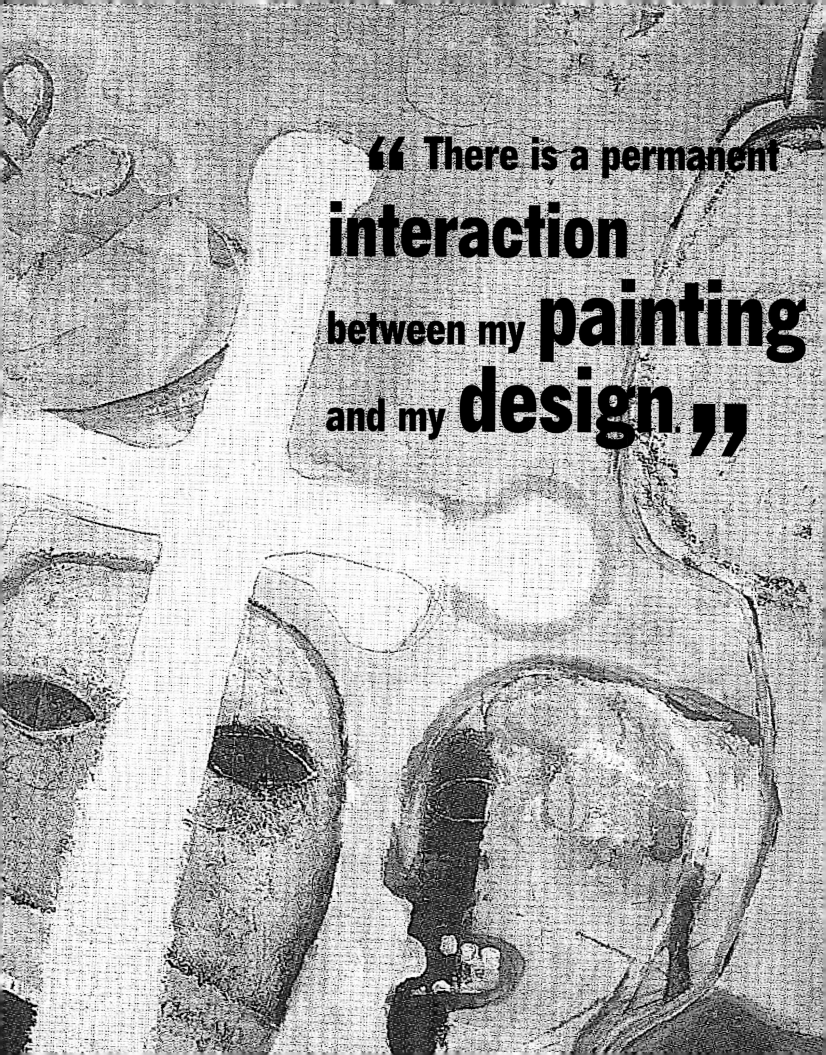

"There is a permanent interaction between my painting and my design."

JAROSLAV MALINA

Jaroslav Malina first graduated in mechanical engineering. In 1964, as a recent graduate of the Drama Faculty of the Academy of Performing Arts in Prague, he was engaged as a stage designer at the Salda Theatre in Liberec, the Czech Republic, where he was part of the core creative team. During his first season he had to design eight productions and embarked upon a career of intense investigation of the possibilities of theatre. Landmark productions include Robinson Jeffers' **Medea** (1974), Ruzante and Gallerova's **What Ruzante Said** (1982), Tankred Dorst's **Merlin** (1988), many Shakespeare plays and the theatrical film **A Magpie in the Hand** (1983). Long-term collaborators include the directors Ivan Balada, Karel Kriz and Miroslav Krobot. Jaroslav Malina is passionately interested in the possibilities of the theatre space and aims to create it afresh in many of his shows, incorporating the audience within the set, combining disparate materials, utilising flowing drapery and transforming the performing space and the actor/performer relationship with great versatility. Throughout his award-winning career as scenographer, Jaroslav Malina has also been active painting, drawing, printmaking and producing ceramics.

INTERVIEW: In my youth I was interested in many things: film directing, literature, philosophy, art and poetry. I was also attracted by technology such as cars and planes; I wanted to be a pilot. When I discovered my limits, such as my lack of aptitude for flying, I concentrated on literature, film and painting. After my studies in art education and languages at Prague's Charles University, I realised that a combination of visual art, literature and especially dramatic literature, philosophy, anthropology and so on, was very interesting. I decided to study at the Academy of Performing Arts under our leading scenographer, Professor Frantisek Tröster.

I began my career with drama, opera and ballet and worked as a resident designer in the Salda Theatre, a beautiful, medium-sized theatre built in the Italian style. As I developed my style I strived to break the conventions and traditional approaches of such theatres. The proscenium-arch stage roused my irritation because of its closed nature and self-complacent historicism. I reacted against the successful, grand scenography of the 1960s and 1970s, such as that of Josef Svoboda and John Bury, which I thought was too decorative and ostentatious. That's why I preferred to design for smaller, experimental and non-traditional stages. It was the time of the now-familiar 'action design' style.

Often in the early part of my career I had to work away from the main centres for political and ideological reasons because of the impact of totalitarian control in Czechoslovakia. When I designed Büchner's grotesque, romantic play **Leon and Lena** in 1976, the production opened in front of the theatre. It was a parody of official celebrations, which the Communists loved so much and, at the same time, it was a play that experimented with an irregular space; it was provocative, inventive and full of action. The final celebration in the play was played with the audience; two narrators communicated with them and moved among them in the auditorium, as well as at the beginning and during the break.

At that time I only had very small budgets to work with but I loved simplicity and the imaginative approach. For my 1982 version of Euripides' **Medea** in a small experimental theatre forum, I had almost nothing. I found some old fabrics, parts of former decorations in other theatres and old tyres. We made costumes with the actors from our supplies at home. Some of our greatest theorists and historians still consider our **Medea** to be the finest Czech production of a Greek drama. Even so, I do not have any problems if I am offered a generous budget.

My process of work is a way of thinking. It is rational, analytical and based on research but it is always corrected by emotion, what I call balancing on the edge. When I have the opportunity, I like to research and prepare a project for a long time. Each time the solution comes with my use of media to express the design visually, mostly with painting, sometimes with a simple drawing. I only like to use models as a way of assuring myself about the right spatial solution. Often the final design solution is arrived at through improvisation during rehearsals. As the rehearsals progress, everything that isn't functional is stripped away. By functional I mean both physically functional – and here I am thinking of the parts of the

LEON AND LENA
By Georg Büchner
Cinohemi, Usti nad labem, Czech Republic, 1976
Directed by Ivan Rajmont

1 Rendering: Costume design for the king
2 Production photo: Act I, The basic set
3 Painting: Act II, Malina's idea for 'The Kingdom of Popo'
4 Painting: The fallen curtain
5 Painting: Act I

1

The design for Büchner's play **Leon and Lena** is a typical example of Malina's use of colourful fabrics to modulate the space of the stage, covering or revealing blooming trees. He contrasted the softness of the fabrics with ugly, grey, worn-out, authentic props, such as old shoes. The costuming was based on a timeless mixture of attributes and accessories, combined with various, sometimes ugly, current materials: "There are some productions on which I want to impress my personal artistic and scenographic ideas and conception of theatre so strongly that I find it absolutely necessary to design the costumes as well." Malina deliberately distorted the theatre space to allow for greater harmony and communication between the actors and the spectators.

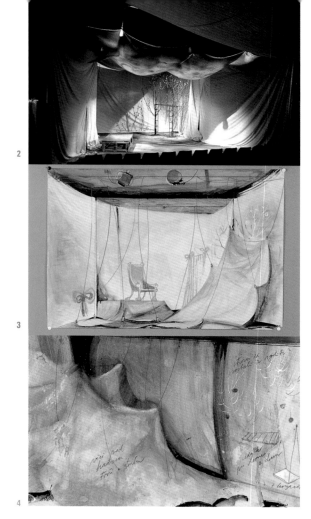

2

3

4

5

1

DON JUAN
By Molière
Municipal Theatre, Zlin, Czech
Republic,1985
Directed by Ivan Balada

1 Drawing: An early solution for
the stage inspired by baroque
garden architecture
2 Production photo: Interlude
between Acts, 'Spatial Ballet'
3 Production photo: Interlude
between Acts, 'Spatial Ballet'
4 Sketch: Costume designs for
the character Don Juan
5 Production photo: Act IV, The
mask of Don Juan
6 Production photo: Act V, Finale,
Don Juan is killed by his own
image

2

3

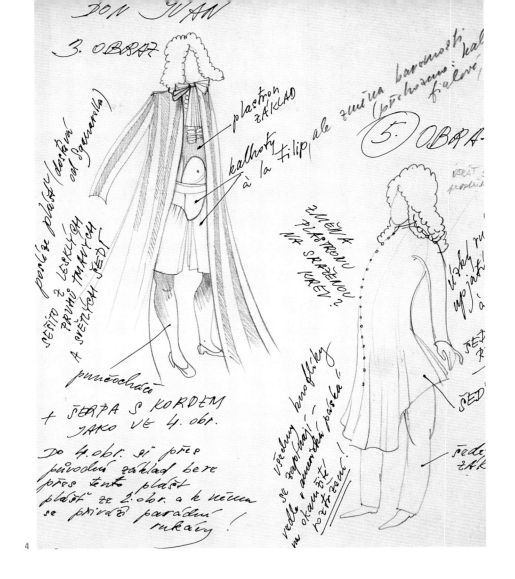

Molière's **Don Juan** had a strong metaphorical concept inspired by baroque garden architecture. Malina then shifted this to a language of irrational concrete objects; abstract constructions of metal and taut fibres that could move and revolve. The costuming combined nudity, fantastic variations on baroque decorativism and contemporary grey, socialist civic suits: "This stylisation was relevant to Molière's classic structure and provided opportunities to emphasise our main theme: hypocrisy and criticism of totalitarian morality." By focusing on the details, Malina also created a design that reflected the film experience of the director, Ivan Balada. At the end a huge mask resembling Don Juan himself was lowered from the grid: "He was metaphorically killed by the hypocrisy of his society. All of the cast played through the holes in that huge mask."

Malina considers his design for **Zajíc, Zajíc** (Hare, Hare) to represent a total synthesis of his work: "The text, a sort of comic, philosophical science fiction, gave us an opportunity to combine the stage and the auditorium, which has been a constant theme of my approach to stage design. I utilised combinations of painted, illusionist details, material structures and funny, inflatable science-fiction plastic objects." Here he used the stage revolve to good effect, also placing a specially-constructed smaller revolve on the apron. At the end of the performance, inflatable objects above the heads of the audience dropped parodic commercial fliers onto their heads, a kind of commentary on free markets.

1

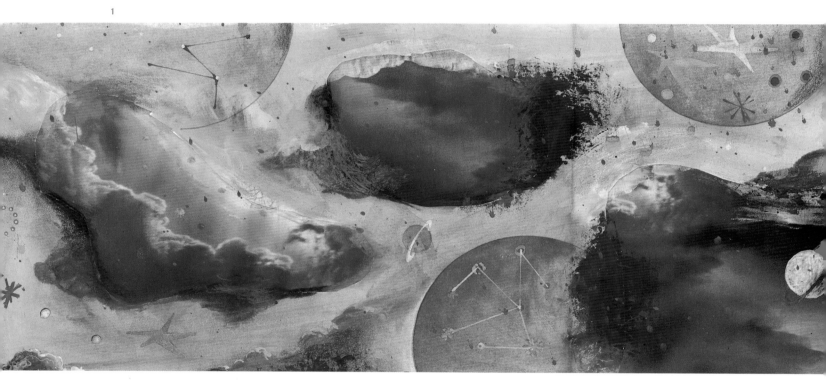

2

3

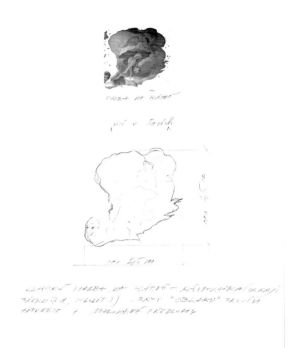

IMAGE VA FLAME

jiet v tavich

*GLIMS IMAGE VA FLAME — RATINUATRA OKRAJE
FEEKU? A, OOLIT 3) · BAYK °OBLAKU° PROVIN
NAPREDIT / MALOVANE PREDLOHY*

*VE FICKA
+ 1/2, 24/12*

4

ZAJIC, ZAJIC
By C. Cerreau
Municipal Theatre, Zlin, Czech
Republic, 1995
Directed by Ivan Balada

1 Painting: Malina's ideas for the
celestial backdrop
2 Production photo: Act II
3 Production photo: Act IV
4 Sketch/collage: The swooping
angel

design that the actor comes into contact with – and emotionally functional, the parts of the stage design that speak to the spectator aesthetically, evoke a certain emotion. And being functional in this way is something quite different from being decorative.

The distinctive qualities of my work are my use of colour, my sense, or feeling, of spatial proportion, my use of materials and structures, my emotionality, my visual mystery and my ability to balance on the edge between rationality and emotionality, authenticity and stylisation. Since the 1970s, I've been convinced that if I use authentic objects, although they may have no great aesthetic value in themselves, they can take on a new significance when they serve a truly functional purpose and interrelate in new and unexpected ways. These authentic objects can create a distinctive, aesthetic whole that has an infinite number of possibilities. In the same way, non-traditional and inappropriate combinations of elements and materials in the costumes can create a clear, powerfully suggestive, aesthetic quality that helps to define the characters and the transformations they undergo. If it were possible I would bring on water, mud, fire – but for a number of reasons this just can't be done; so I work with more acceptable materials, things like real trees, dry leaves and sand. There is going to be a real person moving about on stage, a real person made theatrical by his make-up and costume, and he is going to speak 'real words' elevated by the dramatist into unnatural configurations. And that's what I'm interested in on stage: the relationship between the real and the artificial, the tension that arises when they are combined: a piano among real trees painted white, a picket fence and drapes, a cut-glass chandelier and spotlights.

Colour is also a means for making real objects theatrical. For instance, by painting a real tree I can give it a new presence on stage. Colours aren't always of paramount importance but sometimes they can be used to shift the significance of the physical objects and can actually launch a visual attack on the audience. I also love working with cloth. Of all the materials available, I feel that cloth is the closest to man. After all, since time immemorial, it has been the intermediary between the human body and the world. It is also pliant but can be made stiff; it can be transparent but then opaque; it can flow in smooth folds or lie crumpled up, be beautiful or repellent. I love structures that can be felt under fabric, which call attention to their own existence. Perhaps this has something to do with my long-lasting love of aeroplanes and sailing boats.

In 1982 I had the extraordinary opportunity to produce my total work, for the theatrical film **A Magpie in the Hand**, thanks to the greater budget and materials possibilities offered by a film production. Thanks to the perfect understanding I had with the director Juraj Herz, I created an exaggerated, metaphorical, deliberately theatrically-stylised environment. The story was inspired by medieval moralities but shifted to an imagined future Middle-Ages. My continuing enthusiasm to create tension between natural and artificial, authentic and stylised, real and theatrical, probably reached its climax here. I influenced this film totally

YAGER-TRIKO
VYPISOVANÉ OJETÉ
PŘES NĚJ TÍLKO

ŠNĚROVAČKA

PAŽE OD OLEJE

POTĚRSKÉ RUKAVICE
BEZ PRSTŮ
(KOŽENÉ)

KOŽENÉ OJETÉ KALHOTY

OVINOVAČKY

TĚŽKÉ ŠNĚROVACÍ BOTY

KUKLA

KORPET

KŮŽE

KAPSY

RADĚJI TATO
VERSE NOHAVICE

TĚŽKÉ
ŠNĚROVACÍ
BOTY

2

3

4

5

6

THE INSECT PLAY

By Karel and Josef Capek
National Theatre, Prague, Czech
Republic, 1990
Directed by Miroslav Krobot

1 Drawing: Costumes (previous pages)
2 Drawing: The spiral tunnel and the cloud
3 Production photo: Act I
4 Production photo: Epilogue
5 Drawing: The airplanes
6 Sketch: Costumes and bicycles
7 Sketch: Machines for the parasites in Act II

The philosophical allegory of the **The Insect Play** is usually depicted in a zoomorphic, grotesque manner, using stylised and exaggerated insect elements for costuming and macrovegetation for scenery. "But, for me, the play offers a bitter, sceptical analysis of a purposeless human being, set against a background of natural life." To emulate the structure of nature, Malina used the device of a simple, symmetrical tunnel made of metallic, silver ribs, which was narrowed by exaggerated perspective (1–3). The production was inspired by retro mechanical equipment from the beginning of the 20th century (5–7): early aeroplanes for the butterflies in Act I; tricycles and bicycles for the parasites in Act II and a funny gym and drill equipment for the ants in Act III. "It represents the expansion of technical development then – fast and pragmatic but often lacking humanity. This was extremely relevant to the philosophy of the play. We did not want to use or paraphrase any part of the 'insect world' for costuming, so the costume design was also sort of retro: leather overalls for the airmen-butterflies and gas-masks for the soldiers."

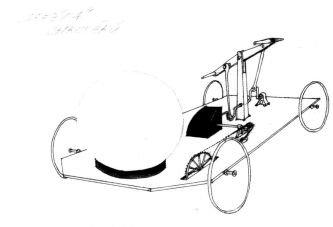

7

1

A MAGPIE IN THE HAND
Barrandov Film Studio, Prague,
Czech Republic, 1982
Filmed at an abandonned quarry
Directed by Juraj Herz

1 Sketch: The main set
2 Painting: The main set
3 Photocopy rendering: Hand-
painting a photocopy of a
location shot
4 Location still: The finished set
before filming
5 Painting: The masks
6 Production photo: The cast
in masks
7 Painting: *The Beauty*, 1980–93,
Jaroslav Malina

2

3

4

5

6

7

This unique film, **A Magpie in the Hand**, based on a medieval story, is perhaps the clearest example of Jaroslav Malina's interest in creating a tension between the real and the theatrical. He created the environment of a future Middle-Ages, employing intense stylisation for the masks and props (1–6). The sources of inspiration were Hieronymous Bosch as well as Pop Art, graffiti, Piero della Francesca and totalitarian garbage. The design was also influenced by his painting at the time (7). "I arranged and prepared everything with the help of my friends and I suggested the shooting sequences. My design functioned like a snowball, increasing and developing itself day by day during two months of filming. I influenced all aspects including lighting, make-up, and choreography."

with my artistic vocabulary, by selecting the location, and by making even the smallest prop. I used an aggressive manner of stylisation for the environment, the costumes, masks, props etc. It provoked an aesthetic shock in 1982 and unfortunately it was banned immediately after completion by the communist censors; it was too wild, strange and provocative. My poster was never printed and when, eight years later, after our Velvet Revolution, the film was finally released, its moment had passed. Nonetheless, after the official premiere in 1990, the critics said that never in the history of Czech film had so much been achieved by a production designer.

In the 1980s I came back to the big theatres, including our National Theatre, without any antagonism, and in the 1990s back to opera and music theatre, with a new sympathy. My relationship towards the proscenium-arch stage is now more tolerant. The necessity of having to work in a large picture frame provokes me to a total use and misuse of pomp, bombast and the theatrical technology and machines available, to make a fuller impression on the audience. One of the productions I worked on at the National Theatre was **The Insect Play** and it is a good example of my return to technology. After a long period of research, the director and I decided upon simple scenery, utilizing the proportions of the National Theatre, mainly its depth. I like to call this scenery a 'tunnel to eternity'. A simple symmetrical tunnel made of metallic, silver ribs, lowered and narrowed by exaggerated perspective, was reminiscent of both the abstraction and the structure of nature. Three versions of a huge cloud, which was coloured, half-destroyed and metallic-armoured, changed the scenery for each of the three Acts. I also used the floor-machinery, hydraulic traps, for the war-situation in Act III. I am not an aficionado of hi-tec but for that production it was purposeful and meaningful.

Occasionally some critics have considered me to be over-dominant. This is paradoxical because I desire dialogue and team-work and I always try to serve the play. Many ideas come out of my head and I can be very stubborn. Yet I have never had a problem with my favourite partners. We might have intense debates about the work but there will always be progress and I also try to encourage open dialogue and mutual respect. I think directors choose me because of my broad range, and because of my ability to change the media and the forms of scenic expression I use according to each production. No matter how different the theatre or the type of drama, you can still recognise Malina's scenery because, they say, of my special flavour or visual magic.

"My work has been **deeply affected by changes** in the technology available for **graphic art**."

WILLIAM DUDLEY

William (Bill) Dudley grew up in London and studied at Central St Martin's School of Art in the 1960s but found his métier through moonlighting at the small Tower Theatre in Islington. His landmark work with director and writer Bill Bryden includes a series of popular and innovative productions in London and Glasgow that created a kind of contemporary, democratic and vernacular British theatre. As well as over 30 shows at the Royal National Theatre, Bill has designed many plays for the Royal Shakespeare Company, The Royal Court Theatre and the West End and has had long-term relationships with many directors. He has designed operas in America and Europe, including Wagner's **Ring Cycle** at Bayreuth and Roman Polanski's musical version of **The Dance of the Vampires**. Bill's many awards include two for his design of the BBC's television production of Jane Austen's novel *Persuasion.* Bill's work is characterised by his enthusiasm for new technologies, by his great respect for history and by the quality of his sketches and rendering.

INTERVIEW: My father was a plumber and my mother worked as a school dinner lady. The notion that I've got such a thrilling job, a job that satisfies all one's various creative urges, is a bonus really. I like to think I'm an artist but I'm very conscious of my father being an artisan; I've always had a good rapport with the stage crews, the stage hands, the carpenters. I need to feel that I'm not betraying my father because, for a very short time just after the war, he was a scene shifter at the Finsbury Park Empire in London.

The reason I got out of painting in the mid-1960s from Central St Martin's School of Art was that it was growing incredibly intolerant of figurative art and of the work of my tutors, Leon Kossoff and Frank Auerbach. So I escaped from art school to the theatre. I would sign in at St Martin's and then go off to the Tower Theatre, a fringe venue up in Islington which I was besotted with and still have an attachment to. One day Leon Kossoff and I went to the National Gallery. We stood in front of the late Rembrandt self portrait and he said, 'Tell me, is there anything in Samuel Beckett that is not there in this painting? The way Rembrandt had piteously looked at himself, is that not what Beckett's plays are all about?' It was a real lesson and I never forgot it. But it was only when Frank Auerbach, looking at my final term exhibition, said, 'there's more of you in the theatre work than in the paintings', that I made my career decision.

In the theatre it is taken for granted that you can paint and draw, and that what you draw has no particular value. One of my models was used for air-rifle target practice by the crew; they didn't think it might mean anything to me, only that the drawings and paintings were a means to another end – the performance. It is utterly unpretentious compared to the art gallery world. Your work is only meant to be a cipher for 'the big thing'. Now I throw drawings down and, compared to a lot of designers, they're quite high standard because that was my background but nobody's reverential about them.

My work has been deeply affected by changes in the technology available for graphic art. In 1973 I bought one of the new airbrushes, the very fine spray-gun that graphic designers use for subtle blends and amazing photographic effects. It revolutionised how I worked in stage design because it gave me the ability to illustrate light in my work. Even though I wasn't a lighting designer, I could work and do sketches for my directors with the lighting as a presence and then show that to lighting designers. It liberated me because I didn't want to work endlessly in flat colours. I needed atmosphere and to be able to paint. In the 1980s came the Agfa enlarger cameras with paper negatives and effects screens, and then in the 1990s came the Macintosh, the one computer at that time for visual people who used the left side of their brain. This gave you immense freedom because you could take any risk you liked. You could even print the thing out on the newly introduced cheap colour printers and then you could distress the paper and then you could put the airbrush over that. Also it's sensationally good for creating the effect of light.

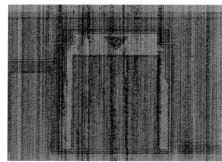

THE HOMECOMING
By Harold Pinter
Royal National Theatre, London, UK, 1997
Directed by Roger Michell

1 Research material: *Study for Crouching Nude*, 1952, Francis Bacon, The Detroit Institute of Arts, Detroit, USA
2 Rendering: Study for the interior based on Bacon's style
3 Research material: A Victorian house
4 Computer rendering: Study of the basic set

Roger Michell wanted the house in **The Homecoming** to embody the horror of two generations of a tortured, dysfunctional family. Dudley remembered helping his father renovate houses in the same part of London; he was inspired by the Victorian Gothic house in the film *Psycho* and by Francis Bacon's paintings: "Bacon's technique was to motion-blur the figures and use a vertical series of lines that made it look as if they were in a streaming rain of blood and tears, like beasts behind bars." (1) Dudley used a series of dark gauzes upon which vertical lines were hand-painted and computer-sprayed. One gauze showed the ghost of the set in 1964 and revealed behind it the decor of the 1930s, when the parents were married (2). Dudley wanted the cut-away set, made from aircraft flooring, to transmit light through its translucent surface: "When their marriage is over at the end, we lit up the back of the set, so the whole house looked like glass – a strangely unnerving effect."

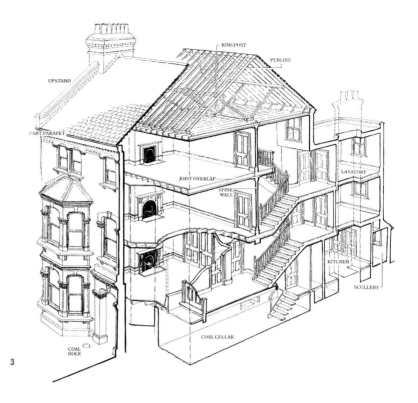

3

4

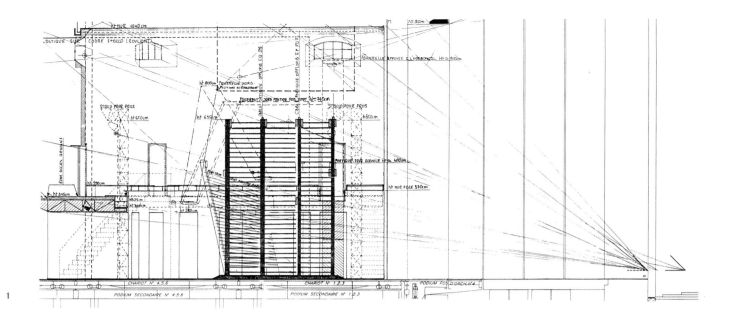

1

2

3

Dudley's inspiration for **Lucia di Lammermoor** was based on the theme of a woman driven to madness by a male, feudal society. The ideas of entrapment and male-dominance were visually rendered in his design of a gladiatorial space where the protagonists could be locked into an arena (2). Dudley then created a gymnasium frame of wall bars and ropes for a gymnastic chorus, one which could also be used for the action (4). "As Lucia goes mad, the whole thing trapezes over and her suitor gets murdered. She sings the madness aria clambering over the gymnasium frame. She's singing about the beautiful hills and the highlands but she's not there; she's imprisoned by her brother." The spartan theme of the military was retained through the elimination of anything superfluous; the only props were a few iron beds and vaulting equipment to evoke the disciplined, masculine environment of the barracks. The chorus became the spectators in the gallery above, their costumes based on the people often found in Edgar Degas' paintings (6).

6

Many directors and theatres still request a model, however. When we're all much more down the road to 3D on computer, that might change but, for now, the fact that each carpenter and scene painter picks up the model that they're looking at and inspects it from every angle several times an hour is significant. I would only be confident if I had the tangible model to offer them. The funny thing about the model is that it appeals to the child in everybody. If you do a beautiful miniaturised model people fall in love with it. It certainly happened on my two shows up in Glasgow, **The Ship** and **The Big Picnic**. They were both written from a one-page outline from Bill Bryden, the director/author, and from that I made the model – and it was used to raise the funding for the whole show.

I began working with Bill Bryden in the mid-1970s in the Cottesloe Theatre at the new National Theatre in London. There was a need for a small experimental space where more risks could be taken and, as luck would have it, there was just enough money to build the basics, nothing too fancy. It was to have been totally in the round but they ran out of money to do the end stage. Bill was made director there and we did six or seven shows together that exploited the building and different forms of theatre. Even though it was the National with all that responsibility, there was a kind of anarchy, a sense that anything goes. One of our greatest successes there was **The Mysteries**, which ran intermittently for nine years, the longest running show they've ever had. I think this was because of the joyous nature of the form: we tried to make the actor/audience relationship closer than even Brecht at his best, enabling the audience to mingle with the actors.

After working for some years at the Cottesloe we were asked to do a project for Glasgow's 'Year of Culture', to be held in 1990. For **The Ship**, Bill's epic play about the lives of the ship builders, we wanted to find an empty industrial space, not a theatre; somewhere where we could build this ship which would be the auditorium, housing 1,100 people. We decided that the presence of the ship would dominate; a ship that might take over two years to build and become an object in these people's lives. It would tower over their houses. The audience sat up on levels; it was kind of a Cottesloe Theatre shaped like a ship in section. For the climax the audience were sent down these 45ft staircases and they would launch the ship – the whole edifice slid away 300ft to the other end of the shed. The set wasn't this decorative, useless afterthought, it was integral; it both housed the play and was the object of the play. It was one of the most emotional things I can ever remember.

The Big Picnic was also staged in the old Harland & Wolff engine shed which had gone to rack and ruin. It follows a group of Glaswegian boys in the First World War. They go through a brief training and then into the hell on the Western front. We wanted to show the realities of mechanised warfare and the dreadful waste of no-man's-land in the 94m-long building we were using. This meant some challenges with the staging and we used this to our advantage. We set up 350 of our audience on a grandstand that tracked alongside the trenches,

LUCIA DI LAMMERMOOR
By Gaetano Donizetti and Salvatore Cammarano
Bastille Opera, Paris, France, 1994
Directed by Andrei Serban

1 Diagram: Side elevation of the set
2 Model: Act I, Scene 2, Lucia alone in the arena
3 Model: Act I, Scene 3, Army barracks
4 Model: Act II, Scene 6, The Arrival of Edgardo
5 Model: Act III, Scene 9, The bridge transformed into 'the hills'
6 Research material: *Jeantaud, Linet and Laine*, 1871, Edgar Dégas, Musée d'Orsay, Paris

Dudley collaborated with Bill Bryden on an epic of ordinary people's experiences called **The Big Picnic**. The story followed a group of young Scottish boys in the First World War: "We wanted to show the realities of mechanised warfare and so presented a completely Godless wasteland, the wasteland of Beckett, where there is no relief from the human condition. You never saw the enemy. We used a powerful array of sound effects and programmed lasers to send a hail of pulses above the heads of the audience. By altering the mirrors on the pulse, you could get an absolute hail of bullets. This was enhanced by dry ice and smoke, which the lasers cut through; the dry ice creates a surface exactly like a misty marsh or a bog. The laser light swapped from red to green so you'd get a sense of marsh gas and of troops being blinded by phosgene gas; they would crawl on their bellies under this laser surface."

THE BIG PICNIC
Promenade Productions, Harland & Wolff Shipyard, Glasgow, UK, 1995
Written and directed by Bill Bryden

1 Production photo: The Angel of Mons (previous left-hand page)
2 Computer rendering: The walking audience is inducted into the battle of the Somme (previous right-hand page)
3 Model: The basic set
4 Drawing: The crane
5 Model: The crane

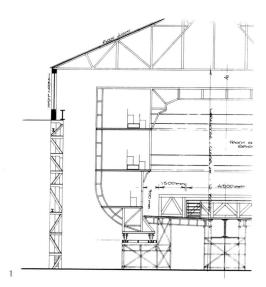

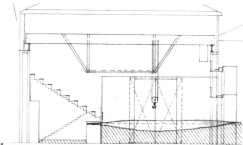

Bryden's play, **The Ship**, about the ship builders of Govan, was set in an old engineering shed on the edge of the river Clyde. The ship itself, which would house the audience as well as provide a setting for the action, was based on a scaled-down Cunard liner. The section was 18.5m long, 14m high and 20m wide and was mounted on a slipway built out of train sleepers on which they laid two railway lines. It was then anchored with the same sort of guy ropes that restrain a real ship on a slipway. The play followed the lives of the men who built this great vessel: "They led rather poor, unhealthy lives but lavished phenomenal skill and care. That was Bill's point; his father was one of these men. We showed the mens' lives, loves, fights, accidents at work, redundancies and so on." At the climax, the ship is launched and the whole edifice slides away, 100 metres down to the other end of the shed and towards enveloping darkness.

THE SHIP
Promenade Productions, Harland
& Wolff Shipyard, Glasgow,
UK, 1990
Written and directed by Bill
Bryden

1 Technical drawing: The ship's
dimensions
2 Photomontage: The shipyard
set after the 'launch' of the ship
auditorium
3 Preliminary sketch: The cast of
actors laying the keel
4 Production photo: Redundant
shipyard workers building the ship

1

The principles of perspective, c1780
Pen and ink and watercolour, with some bodycolour

Anonymous

2

The setting for **Maria Stuart** began with the metaphor of an
elaborate gilded cage, with all the deadly notions of the political,
Machiavellian court. "We thought paper was her downfall – she
was trapped when she sent anti-Elizabeth messages – so we
abandoned the idea of a masonry prison and kept with the
diagonal movement, which we took from a treatise on perspective
(1), and the Claude Lorraine painting." (2) The walls of the palace
were covered in trompe l'oeil drawings which continued the theme
of the sinister, and the slashings reflected the fashion for slashed
doublets and the lies in the world of the court, like Hamlet's
Elsinore (4, 5). A sundial also became the focus of the ground
plan: "There's a lot of Renaissance philosophy about the sun
creeping round and we all go nearer to our grave."

3

MARIA STUART
By Friedrich Schiller
Royal National Theatre, London,
UK, 1996
Directed by Howard Davies

1 Research material: *The
Principles of Perspective*, c1780
2 Computer rendering: Dudley's
rendering for the set based on
the principles of perspective with
Claude Lorraine's *Landscape with
Psyche outside the Palace of
Cupid* at the centre
3 Model: Act II
4 Computer rendering: Wallpaper
trompe l'oeil motif
5 Computer rendering: 'Claude
Lorraine' swag over the bookcase

following the action. Led by the skirl of bagpipes, the emotional charge of the piper getting up and walking forward and these people going to almost certain death was tremendous. We used a massive, motorised crane that ran on rails and towered high above. Then we suspended the bandstand for the musicians under the crane and on the big crane hook stood this trapeze artist we called the Angel of Mons. Troops had hallucinogenic visions of angels; many imagined they wouldn't be killed because of their guardian angel. She had a harness with a small hook and would snap-hook a soldier. Then she'd lift him like a 19th-century war statue and take him away. The setting became a kind of spiritual landscape expressing what some of the soldiers still believed in and showing something of what they experienced.

I call this kind of setting the 'dream space'. What I call the dream space is something initiated by Inigo Jones for post-Shakespearean theatre, the space created by the Italian theatres of the Renaissance. A lot of people say that theatre was in decline then because of the decadence and the delight of the court in Inigo Jones' spectacle and poor old Ben Johnson was raving 'It's only a picture gallery. What has happened to my words? I'm being upstaged by these monsters and beasts!' Well, if you deny the visual aspect of theatre you may as well also deny the importance of cinema. The notion that the inner language of pictures has no place in the theatre is a nonsense. What Inigo Jones brought to theatre was the idea that you had a performance arena where the action takes place and then upstage you had a pictorial space where you can advance the passage of time and you can break the laws of physics. In the performance area you're in real time and you obey the laws, and in the 'dream space' you can play the spiritual dimension of the story, as I did with the Angel of Mons. I like this ability to play with the two realities.

I only started looking at alternative forms of staging, at 3D, when I started working with Bill Bryden at the Cottesloe in the round, and I realised what a magnificent form had been lost. If you look at the paintings of Watteau depicting the court revels of the late-18th century, at the people in brilliant silks living in a kind of Arcadian illusion, he shows the proscenium arch and through it a room about the same size as the Cottesloe. In that space he paints quite artificial trees, dream trees, a vision of a kind of paradise garden. I like to have both, a thrusting stage which is in our world, as well as that extra pictorial space where the actors can go off into their dream world. I would love to write a treatise on that; the power and development of painting and theatre and how they both echo each other and learn from each other – and how they both coincide in cinema. Because that's what the public finally needed or demanded, a means of showing the world in all its complexity, relatively effortlessly.

For the musical, **The Dance of the Vampires**, based on Polanski's 1968 film, Dudley planned a monochromatic set which offered heightened supernatural realism, like Melies' early films. His inspiration was Gothic architecture combined with the more extreme, decadent art nouveau forms which sprang from it: "If you look at the detailing, you can see elegant long spines of stone with tendrils of flowers that grow out of it. It's all about organic form, which is exactly what art nouveau has. I also wanted to make it all faintly disgusting, using mother of pearl varnishes and glistening dampness everywhere, and to pick up on Polanski's delight in this Edgar Allen Poe world of vaults and caskets and that sense of eternity. The biggest moment is when all the graves fly in for the scene where they open up on the night of the ball and the cast emerge. It's one of the best technical moments I've ever had a hand in and the music was big enough for it."

THE DANCE OF THE VAMPIRES
Music by Jim Steinman and
Michael Kunze
United Vienna Theatre, Vienna,
Austria, 1994
Directed by Roman Polanski

1 Computer rendering: The graveyard
2 Computer rendering: The guest bedroom
3 Computer rendering: The coffin scene
4 Computer rendering: The approach to the vampire's castle
5 Computer rendering: The labyrinth

Cleo, Camping, Emmanuelle and Dick was a celebration of the English Carry On films: "They're a kind of vulgar, fun celebration of the absurdities of English life. There was a desire to make these films bright and cheerful; the colouring in the later films is very crude. The Carry On line goes from sources like Hogarth through to the great English comics like *Beano* and *Dandy*, to some Beatles films and songs, to the English comic actor Benny Hill and so on." Dudley related this to an area of under-celebrated painting in Britain, known as commercial art applications; the applied art of railway and underground tube posters and the Shell Guides and adverts: "British painters like Nevison, Wadsworth, Ravilious, Cook, Hillier and Newton who show great observational integrity, looking for the poetic in the ordinary. They had a romantic eye for the essence of things, a sense of pleasure in what they did and offered a slightly easy-listening kind of surrealism. This inspired my designs."

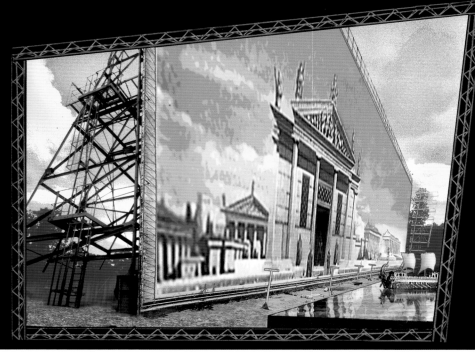

3

CLEO, CAMPING, EMMANUELLE AND DICK
Royal National Theatre, London, UK, 1998
Written and directed by Terry Johnson

1 Research material: *The Villages of England*, 1932, Brian Cook
2 Research material: *The Spirit of London*, 1937, Brian Cook
3 Computer rendering: Act I, stretched backcloths depicting a Pinewood backlot

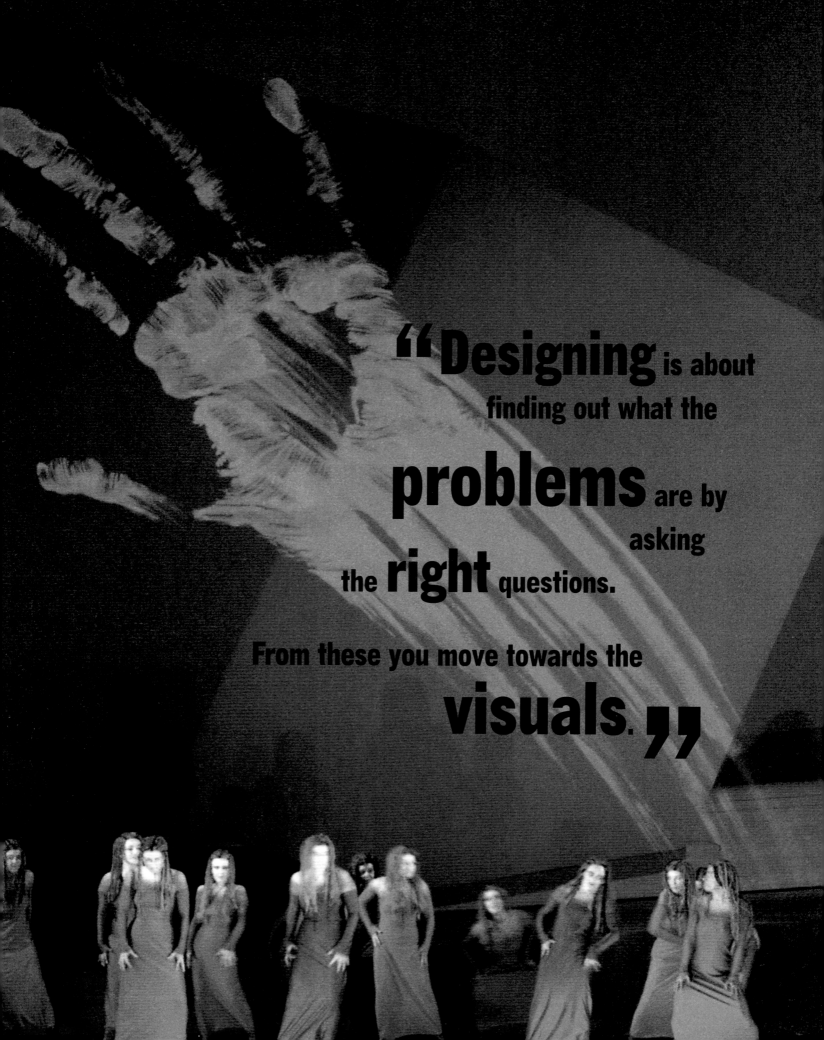

"**Designing** is about finding out what the **problems** are by asking the **right** questions.

From these you move towards the **visuals.**"

MARIA BJÖRNSON

Maria Björnson was born in Paris. She went to London for her higher education and studied at the Byam Shaw School of Art and at the Central St Martin's School of Art and Design. Her stage design work was grounded in rigorous repertory training and team work at Glasgow Citizen's Theatre. Björnson made her mark early in her career with David Pountney; their stagings of Janáček's operas led to acclaim and encouraged the realisation that Janáček had created perhaps the greatest 20th-century opera cycle. This ability to serve work with fidelity and inspiration has led to an international career in opera and theatre. Of all her work, the best known is her staging and costumes for **The Phantom of the Opera** which has been staged around the world. Maria Björnson has sustained good working relationships with many directors and has designed plays, musicals, operas, dance and ballet. She has won many set and costume awards including the 1990 *Observer* 'Experts' Expert' and 'The Designers' Designer' in recognition of her contribution to theatre design, as well as the Silver Medal Prague Biennale for the **Janáček Cycle**.

INTERVIEW: When I was 12 the painter Victor Pasmore came to see my work and said 'You should be a theatre designer'. I was an only child and used to do lots of drawings of characters going on journeys and having adventures. I think he thought it was similar to the process of costume design. I then did two years pre-diploma at Byam Shaw followed by three years of theatre design at Central St Martin's School of Art in London under Ralph Koltai. From there I was offered a job at Glasgow Citizen's Theatre. It was a wonderful place to be as you either sunk or swam. I did 16 shows in a year and a half. It was two-weekly and three-weekly rep so we would open a show on a Friday and have to have the next show designed by the Monday. It was very good training because there was no model – you just had to think in terms of ideas which was quite frightening. Rep teaches you throwaway, everything has to be done so fast – you just have to get on with it.

Serving an apprenticeship through rep was an excellent way of getting started in design although it can be lonely at the beginning. At Glasgow Citizen's Theatre I was lucky to continue working with Sue Blane whom I had met at Central St Martin's – we bounced ideas off each other which gave us the confidence to make mistakes and find our way. They were fantastic early days. We worked on quite a mix of plays including pantomime which was great to have done before coming down to London. Working on the Janáček operas with David Pountney, whom I had met at Glasgow Citizen's Theatre, was an incredible opportunity, and a great career prospect, although I wish it had happened later because I was still grappling with the medium of designing. I became more comfortable while working on **The Makropulos Affair** and **The Cunning Little Vixen**.

Designing is finding out what the problems are by asking the right questions. It's not about searching for visuals, it's about searching for questions that give you the right answers – from these you move towards the visuals. For example, with **The Cunning Little Vixen** one of the challenges was to get the adults to move freely; another was how to show the cycle of the seasons. My response was to do a shorthand for nature, so what I ended up with was a slab like a sort of rolling hill where the action would take place. In fact, when the set arrived the adults started saying 'we cannot work on this', but then the children arrived and just rushed on to it and rolled about, went through the trapdoors and were having a terrific time. After a while the adults were rather shamefaced and started tumbling about as well, using the set in a much freer way.

Showing the transition from one season to another demonstrates how direction and design often have to work hand in hand. It starts with Summer, then moves to Autumn, then Winter, Spring and back to Summer. So the Summer scene was set outside with trees and for the next transition I had an animal walking across

KATYA KABANOVA
By Leos Janacek
Royal Opera House, London,
UK, 1994
Directed by Trevor Nunn

1 Research material: *Despair*,
1893, by Edvard Munch, Munch
Museum, Oslo
2 Research material: *Puddles*,
1952, by M.C. Escher
3 Production photo: Act III, Scene
2, Before Katya jumps from the
cross
4 Production photo: Act I, Scene 2,
Sewing the bridal veil

"For **Katya Kabanova**, Trevor Nunn wanted to emphasise the call of the Volga river. He was interested in a set where you didn't really know where the water or the sky started or where the earth was. I looked at Munch skies for Katya's madness and at Escher's pictures of mud tracks with water reflections in them." One of the problems that Björnson encountered was how to bring on the church as the music continues through scene changes. She wanted to do something that could collapse and disappear when Katya kills herself and also make a point about how she kills herself, leaving a fallen cross (3). The production ends with a bridal procession; the front curtain was like a wedding veil and had the lace at the bottom. It was used earlier in the opera when the three women were doing embroidery on a hot night on another wedding veil (4).

1

WITCHES
PUSH
CUBE ROUND
TO REVEAL L. MACBETH

ACT I·1 INTO ACT I·2

BLUE   BLUE

3

BLUE
BLUE
BLUE

OUTSIDE PARK
NEAR MACBETHS
CASTLE ACT II·

BLOOD RUNNING
DOWN CUBE AS
BANQUO + FLEAN
MEET THEIR END

5

WITCHES ACT III SC·I

GREEN

BLUE GAUZE
+ GREEN HAND
SYMBOLIZING

WOODS +
WITCHES
MOVEMENTS

WITCHES
ENTER THRO
ELASTIC FR
STAGE STI
HAND AND

7

BLUE
PALE GREY
OPEN
PALE
GREY
BLUE

GREEN CYKE

GREEN CYKE

ACT IV·4
BATTLE

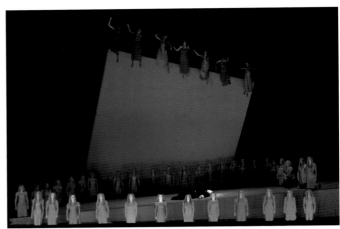

2

4

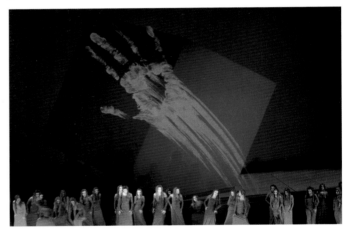

6

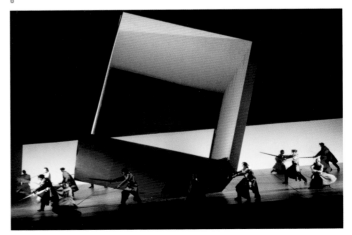

8

For this production of Verdi's **Macbeth**, Björnson informed Graham Vick that she saw a great square, like in Mecca. They opted for a cube which was placed at an angle, off-centre. The revolving cube was associated with the turning of fate and its heaviness was associated with oppression. The production was also colour-coded throughout. In Act I the cube represented the weight of the world on the chorus; it revolved to reveal Lady Macbeth (1, 2). The surface was then used to reveal Banquo's blood (3, 4) and the hand that was to represent Burnham Wood as well as the hand of the witches who conjure up the wood (5, 6). During Act III the refugees had bits of green in their costumes, like bits of cracked earth; these co-ordinateed with the colours for the battle (7, 8).

MACBETH
By Guiseppe Verdi
La Scala, Milan, Italy, 1997
Directed by Graham Vick

1 Storyboard: Act I, Scene 1 into Scene 2
2 Production photo: Act I, Scene 1 into Scene 2
3 Storyboard: Act II, Scene 2, The conspirators
4 Production photo: Act II, Scene 2, The conspirators
5 Storyboard: Act III, Scene 1, The witches
6 Production photo: Act III, Scene 1, The witches
7 Storyboard: Act IV, Scene 4, The battle
8 Production photo: Act IV, Scene 4, The battle

the stage with an old carrier bag, dropping these leaves into the yard so you knew you were in Autumn. Then, after the interval, we covered the set with these silks which were like snow and which also provided a hiding place for the vixen when she was meeting the badger. For the transition into Summer the moles came on again and pulled the silks down through the holes in the set. It was very simple. After that the cast came on with these Chinese umbrellas which we adapted to fold backwards and, as they popped open, they would become these huge flowers. That was how we segued from one scene into another. At college Ralph Koltai said that scene changes are one of the most satisfying things you can do as a theatre designer. Very often the scene changes are what sets the mood, not the scene itself. It's how you arrive from one to the other that makes a huge impact.

If I'm doing a play then I'm much more text orientated, and what I do is make a storyboard where I'll write out various columns depending on what the piece needs. For instance what I've done with Chekhov's **The Cherry Orchard** at the Royal National Theatre is have a column headed 'Set description'; then I've got 'Season', 'Time of day', 'Sound', 'Entrances and Groupings', 'Prop details', 'Costume details' and 'Remarks'. If it's not too detailed I'll try and get it all onto one big sheet. It gives me an idea of how many people are on stage at any one time – I can look through my text and refer immediately back to the piece. In 'Set description' I make a note of what every character says about the set. 'Prop details' is any description that a character gives about something else and likewise with the 'Costume details'. This method lets me know exactly where I am. I don't need to go back to the play because I have a clear and detailed idea. It's taken me a long time to come to this way of doing it but it does help. When I get a little bit further with the design I like having a column of 'Things to do', so I know exactly where I am and how much more we've got to make.

You find the dynamic from the text, not from a fantasy idea that you have – you go to the main source. With **The Cherry Orchard** it's all about entrances and exits, it's about throwaway remarks, so the minute I came to that idea I designed lots of doors because you can't just have two – there has to be a space where everybody is coming and going. However, with an opera or musical it is much more to do with the mood of the music, so I write down the feeling of the music, what segues into what. It's different with a play because the actors can pace themselves, whereas with an opera, musical or ballet you've got to follow what is happening. People think it's liberating to be able to do anything but it's not. What you're trying to do is hone yourself down and reduce and reduce until you discover exactly what it is you're trying to resolve.

The Marriage of Figaro is a typical instance where you're really stepping back with the design. It's about the momentum of the piece so what I tried to do was build momentum into the scene changes and show the wonderful way that Mozart drives forward. I attempted to give the whole thing a kick with each change. Figaro is all about hiding and being surprised as well as class. The idea

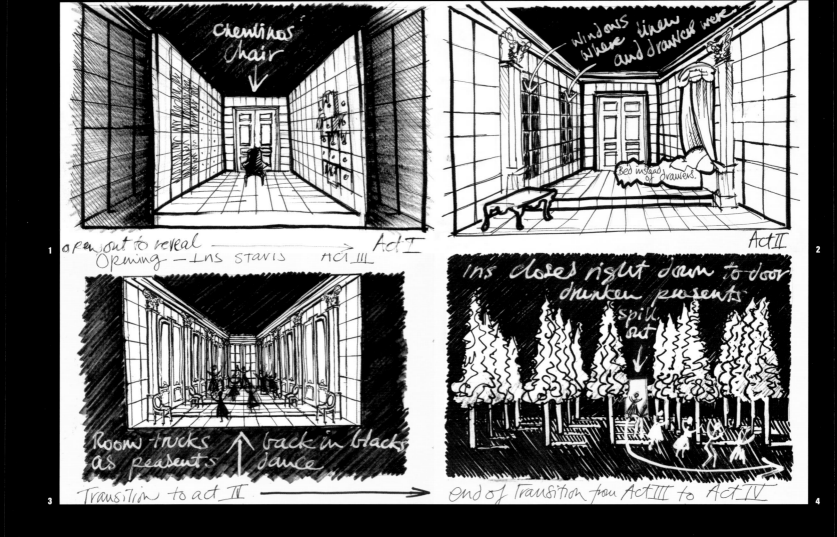

1 · open out to reveal — Opening — Ins starts   Act I
  Act III
Chenlinos' chair

2 · Windows where linew and drawers were   Act II
  Bed instead of drawers.

3 · Room trucks as peasants   back in blacks dance
  Transition to act IV ————————➤

4 · Ins closes right down to door drunken peasants "spill out"
  end of Transition from Act III to Act IV

8

9

10

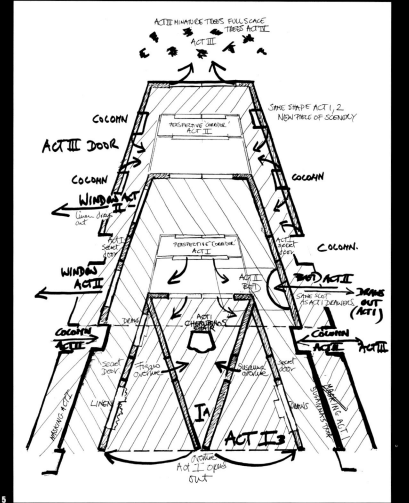

ACT III MINATURE TREES FULL SCALE
TREES ACT IV
ACT III

SAME SHAPE ACT I, 2
NEW PIECE OF SCENERY

COLOHN
ACT III DOOR
COLOHN
PERSPECTIVE 'CORRIDOR'
ACT II
COLOHN

WINDOW ACT II
linen drops out

ACT I
secret door
PERSPECTIVE 'CORRIDOR'
ACT I
ACT I
secret door
COLOHN.

WINDOW
ACT I
ACT II
BED
BED ACT II
SAME SPOT
AS ACT I DRAWERS
DRAWS
OUT
(ACT I)

COLOHN
ACT II
DRAWS
ACT I
CHERUBINOS
CHAIR
COLOHN
ACT II
ACT III

MASKING ACT II
secret door
Figaro
overture
Susanna
overture
secret door
MASKING ACT I
SUSANNA'S DOOR

LINEN
IA
DRAWS

ACT II 3

overture
Act I opens
out

5

6

7

11

THE MARRIAGE OF FIGARO

Music by Wolfgang Amadeus
Mozart and Lorenzo da Ponte
The Grand Theatre, Geneva,
Switzerland, 1989
Directed by Nicholas Hytner

1 Storyboard sketch: Act I
2 Storyboard sketch: Act II
3 Storyboard sketch: Act III
4 Storyboard sketch: transition
from Act III to Act IV
5 Technical drawing: The layout
and positioning of the scenes
6 Research material: 28, 1601,
Jan Vredeman de Vries
7 Research material: 29, 1601,
Jan Vredeman de Vries
8 Production photo: Act I
9 Production photo: Act II
10 Production photo: Act III
11 Production photo: Act IV

Björnson took her inspiration for this production from a 16th-century book on perspective (6, 7). "**The Marriage of Figaro** is like a technical drawing; it's crisp, sharp and clear, there's no room for error. It's all about flats, hiding and being surprised as well as about class; doors that lock and so on; so it has to have real rooms, it can't be just anywhere. We thought that the door should be downstage but the first point of view was to show that a wedding was about to happen and that it was really the two of them against the world." To start with, the set was a small room which grew into a bigger room (1–3, 8–10) that had to be high up because Caribena falls out of the window. Towards the end, the three rooms merge into one great hall. In the final, unbuttoned scene, 18 pine trees emerged and the peasants drunkenly spilt outside (11).

THE CUNNING LITTLE VIXEN

By Leoš Janáček
Welsh National Opera and Scottish Opera, 1980
Directed by David Pountney

1 Drawing: Costumes for the hens and cockerel
2 Drawing: Costumes for the birds
3 Production photo: The hens, vixen and cockerel
4 Model: Act I, Scene 2, The humans' courtyard
5 Model: Act II, Scene 1, Winter
6 Model: Act II, Scene 2, Summer
7 Model: Act III, Scene 1, Autumn

In **The Cunning Little Vixen** Björnson decided that she didn't want the birds to fly because this had been done often before: "I thought, 'Why not put them in armchairs so that they look like humans? The armchairs would be green, have antimacassars on them and have bags all around where the birds have got knitting and things.'" (2) Björnson discovered a series of solutions to her challenges so that the whole production became light, simple and direct, assuming the clarity of an unsentimental folk tale. To represent the seasons she decided to do a shorthand for nature and ended up with a slab, like a rolling hill on which the performers could move freely (4–7).

4

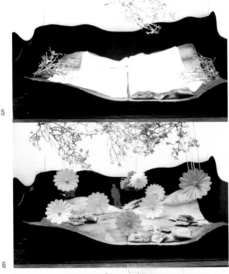

5

6

7

was that it started with a sort of corridor. You saw Figaro and Susanna on either side and as they walked the back wall moved backwards, so the space transformed into a larger room. So finally we're in the Great Hall where the wedding takes place; this was made up of the three previous rooms which had all merged together. As it went all the way back, 18 pine trees came up from underneath and all the peasants spilled drunkenly outside. That's how we made that scene change. We used the fact that with Mozart people can dress up, they can do what they want, they're all drunk, anything can happen and that's why it had a totally different visual feel as well.

One of the biggest problems with designing is that you have to do your bit so far in advance. If you're doing an opera or a ballet, it can be quite circumscribed and you can be more specific. With an opera the performers have got a voice, you're putting your design over them. In a play you're underneath them, supporting them from the bottom up. Some opera performers can arrive six days beforehand – they've done it ten times before and all they want to know is where they'll stand; others will be there four weeks before rehearsal. A play develops more in rehearsal, so you have to be a bit more nebulous. Sometimes with a play things can completely *volte-face* because people discover things that weren't previously discussed with the director. You have to be able to accommodate that and hopefully have the budget for it. Each new project is different for both the director and the designer. Sometimes the director has an absolute idea and you follow them, other times you have the idea and they follow you, but the best approach is when you both talk about what the actual piece means and bounce ideas off each other, without any visual references.

I'm very clear about who I'm designing for – I'm doing it for the audience. You have to look at the audience versus the piece, so if it's a piece that's quite well known then you have more freedom. If it's something that's not so well known then it is your duty to show the piece off for the first time and be true to it. I also think you must never talk down to your audience; that's a big mistake, especially with musicals. A lot of people do – they make things into easy listening and easy viewing, which isn't right.

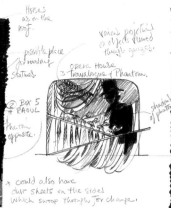

Horses as on the roof.

possible place for rendering Statues.

various projection of objects viewed through gauges.

Opera House 3 Travalogue + Phantom.

② Box 5 + Raoul

→ Phantom opposite.

shadow of phantom

* could also have dust sheets on the sides which swoop through for change.

① SUGGESTION - lots of fallen drapes - gauges Auction high up - objects handed to auctioneer + chandelier in Pit masked by gauze —

④ Chandelier goes up out of pit (Do not like drapes at the top - but like it in the pit)

PROSCENIUM ARCH SEQUENCE —
Act I.
1) auction
2) Box 5 + Raoul.
3) Opera house comes to life — Travalogue.
4) Chandelier goes up —
5) Transformation to gala
6) Box 5 + Raoul.
7) 'Phantom of the Opera'
8) On the Roofs of Paris
9) Phantom — vis-a-vis Chandelier.
10) Chandelier

Act II
1) Possible use of boxes for Opera Ball?
2) "   "   for Policemen
3) Same treatment of Pros for descent to Cats comes

conductor upstage —

as orchestra goes back down

Curtain call theatre switches back to front several times

Chandelier a swag curtain with a drop curtain

⑤ Transformation to gala Orchestra rises up out of pit brilliantly lit. Kristin could go up with them.
* and or the back lights up to reveal auditorium —
chandelier + other lamps around auditorium light up.

⑦ PHANTOM OF THE OPERA - COULD USE gauzes from 'operas' and project on them
DROS ARCH SHOULD CHANGE / REVOLVE V. FRIGHTENING LIT FROM INSIDE STATUES.

⑧ SUR LES TOITS.... LARGE GARGOIL DESCENDS + PHANTOM ON TOP - R + K COME UP TO MEET THEM. SAME MECHANISM AS AUCTIONEER IC. CEILING + AUDITORIUM STARS.

⑨) Phantom stays where he is and alts the Chandelier down — or —

or — 9)

10) Chandelier Crashing — see drawings for Crashing Chandelier

1

2

The Phantom of the Opera posed many challenges for Björnson from the mask to the need to create a sense of depth on stage when there was really not enough room to accommodate a staircase. At their first meeting, Harold Prince said that he wanted dark Turkish corners, drapes flooding very heavily onto the floor and people running out into blackouts. The Paris Opera House was an inspiration; it has a lake in its basement and many other curiosities. Ben Carré, who designed the Lon Chaney film, had worked there and used it to influence the look of the film. "What I loved was the big circular descent that was like going down into the subconscious. I started off with a straight staircase (5). From there I got the idea of the lantern that has striations on it and from there we got the idea of the striations as a way of lighting the whole thing. I had seen a picture of Venice that had reflections in the water and that's where I got the idea for the candles. Each candle comes up from its own little trap." (4)

4

THE PHANTOM OF THE OPERA
By Andrew Lloyd Webber,
Charles Hart and Richard Stilgoe
Her Majesty's Theatre, London,
UK, 1986
Directed by Harold Prince

1 Storyboard: Act 1 Overture
2 Storyboard: Act 1, Rooftop and chandelier crash
3 Drawing: Chandelier
4 Production photo: Act 1, Lake
5 Drawing: Act 1. Journey into lair

"I always think of the **actor** when I **design my stages**"

JC
SERRONI

José Carlos (known as JC) Serroni, in the absence of Brazilian training courses for scenographers, studied Higher Mathematics for a year and then architecture at the University of São Paulo. During his university years he became a 'multiple artist', painting, developing scenography, and working with samba schools during carnival. He spent six years working in a state-owned Educational TV Network where he met Antunes Filho and other great theatre directors but he grew frustrated with the short-term industrial nature of the medium. Since that time he has been exceptionally busy and prolific, working intensively as Head of Design at Filho's Centre for Theatre Research SESC (CPT) for over a decade. He has achieved a worldwide reputation for his work with Grupo Macunaima, especially for **North Side Paradise**, adapted from plays by Nelson Rodrigues. His other achievements include advising on the building of new theatres across Brazil, as he still practices as a theatre-specialist architect; leading the Brazilian delegation to the Prague Quadriennale scenography exhibition, where he won the Golden Triga in 1995; creating and leading the Espaço Cenográfico in São Paulo in 1998 as a dedicated environment for researching and developing scenography and, of course, designing productions. Serroni is now both a leading scenographer and a key figure in the development and future of theatre and scenography in Brazil.

INTERVIEW: At university, I continued with my amateur acting and had the opportunity of being Flávio Império's pupil during the course. After graduating as an architect and following my experiences with educational and commercial television, the theatre fascinated me much more. In 1986 and 1987 I realised that, as a freelance, I was spreading myself too thinly over too many activities that did not represent continuity; it was all too quick and superficial. This near-crisis coincided with going to Prague for the design Quadriennale for the first time, to show some work as part of the Brazilian delegation. That was the first contact I had with what was done in scenography outside my country.

When I came back to Brazil, I wanted to focus my work on a denser, deeper project. Coincidentally I was contacted by Antunes Filho, who directed a Centre for Theatre Research SESC (CPT) that was greatly respected. I told him about my concerns and we started to work together. I created a scenography nucleus within the research centre, for the purpose of researching design languages, to train young scenographers and to carry out a much more integrated work; not for immediate results – projects took one to two years before going on stage – but for focusing on the process. Some of the most important work in my career was carried out with Antunes Filho at CPT, including **New Old Story**, **Salvation Path** and **Dracula and other Vampires**. Eleven years later I decided to leave the CPT to get to know other possibilities and to focus my work more on the scenographic universe. I created the Espaço Cenográfico (Scenographic Space), based on my experience at the CPT, although it is more open, encouraging the exchange of experiences, research and access to my library of theatre and design books.

Scenography in Brazil is still in its infancy; it started to be a spatial language around the 1960s. Before that, our scenography was limited to painted backdrops and a few pieces of furniture and props. The change was initiated by scenographers such as Flávio Império, Gianni Ratto, Hélio Eichbauer and Lina Bo Bardi. Nearly 20 years later, I found things already a little different and tried to improve on the ideas of the previous generation. I had private lessons with Flávio Império, my university teacher. I admired his lean work, the search for alternative materials – he used lots of cloth in unusual ways – and, above all, his passion for the craft.

As an artist, the work of a scenographer is usually more rational and objective: he builds things. But I think that everything that is translated physically on stage is the rendition of a creative process which comes from a posture that must be informed by an understanding of humanity. I always think of the actor when I design my stages. When I materialise a space for the scene, it is conceived to accommodate the actors' movements. My premise is that the actor is the centre of the show; the other languages used in the theatre must evolve around him. Scenography is born with the process of the production. By maturing day to day, it transforms itself, grows life and humanises itself.

NEW OLD STORY
Adapted from the story of Little Red Riding Hood
Macunaima Group, Teatro Anchieta, São Paulo. Brazil, 1991
Directed by Antunes Filho

1 Production photo: Act I
2 Model: Act I
3 Storyboard: Act I

1

2

New Old Story used an invented language called 'Phonemol',
later used in **Dracula and other Vampires** (see pp108–111).
Serroni describes it as one of the most satisfying collaborations he
has ever had with a director. "For this story we wanted a scenography that evoked the cosmos. The hope was that the public would
'dream awake' so they would drift into another state of
consciousness and embark on our journey. The play was on stage
for five years and visited several cities in the world; very often our
intention was achieved." Besides the planets, the scenario was
intended to be reminiscent of childhood soap bubbles and the
black and white striped floor recalled children's sports and games
and offered a discipline for movement around the stage. "It was
a scenography in the air; the stage and floor were free for
the actors."

Salvation Path deals with religious fanaticism. At the end of the show the whole community, following their religious leader Joaquim, is in a clearing in the Brazilian jungle, jumping in order to take flight and get to heaven. A big confusion contained in the plot gets the police, tipped by dissidents, to surround the multitude of fanatics; contradictory orders make them shoot on all sides and kill everybody. This production coincided with a massacre in Carandiru, a prison in the city of São Paulo, where 111 inmates were murdered. Street children were killed in front of the Candelária church in Rio de Janeiro and a group of Indians were killed in Amazonia. Unfortunately, things continue years later in prisons for teenagers or in clashes between the police and the Sem-Terra, 'the landless', and so on. **Salvation Path** was a manifesto to denunciate all of these massacres but it was not a pamphleteering play, nor was it engaged or realistic. It was poetic, subtle, even delicate.

As the public came in, the whole cast was standing within very coarse funerary urns. These were 12 vertical boxes under faint light. As the play started, in a blackout, the cast came out of the urns and these were suspended. The scene was copied exactly from a newspaper photo showing the dead in Vigário Geral slum, thrown in boxes, one next to the other. A large forest was indicated by about 130 eucalyptuses, each 8–9m high. Half of them were real because they were used; people climbed them, held them, leaned against them. The others were false; they were worked-over plastic piping tubes. A central clearing was created and the movement of the play took place between or behind the vertical lines created by the trees. At times they were reminiscent of prison bars. People were caged up in their nearly paranoid world of abandonment.

The production had much impact without being blunt or crass; that moved the public and it moved me too. I think it was one of the plays I did that I like the most, along with **North Side Paradise**. It showed me where theatre language can get, how strong and subjective it is, capable of touching the lives of people, making them ponder about the world.

I always use scale models to work. I can now solve scenography directly in the three-dimensional process. I can think scenography through the model, sometimes without the intermediate drawing step. It is the most useful tool for everyone involved in the process. I also use other tools: technical drawings for the execution, at times; perspectives for certain jobs and, when we have many scenes, a storyboard to visualise scene after scene. In some cases, though rare, we experiment with scenography using prototypes on a 1:1 scale. Computers help with certain things, especially in the technical aspect – in drawing, designing the blueprints or, sometimes, to visualise three-dimensional spaces and get different view angles. A benefit I have in the theatre is a longer time to build the set, so as to be able to correct or alter details on the stage. I think the theatre and, consequently, scenography are living things, which are altered day to day; they become rich just moments before the opening.

Salvation Path reveals Serroni's concern to make an environment within which an ensemble of performers can create a show. This kind of approach works especially well when there is a body of actors who have a unified and often highly physical approach to performance. The trees rising into the roof of the theatre create an epic scale for this single set, a scale that is suitable for presenting the plight of people who are struggling against the odds.

SALVATION PATH
By Jorge Andrade
Macunaima Group, Teatro Anchieta,
São Paulo, Brazil, 1993
Directed by Antunes Filho

1 Model: The basic set
2 Antunes Filho (left) and JC Serroni
(right) inspecting the model
3 Production photo: Act I
4 Production photo: Act I
5 Production photo: Act I

Serroni's influences for **Dracula and other Vampires** included vampire books, poetry, and countless films, among them *The Cabinet of Dr Caligari* by Robert Wiene, *Metropolis* by Fritz Lang and *Mesa Verde*, the film on ballet by Kurt Loos, as well as a series of films on German Nazism by Leni Riefenstahl. The storyboards show the influence of comics such as *Tales from the Crypt*, *Mad* magazine and the drawings by Crepax. Serroni says that "**Dracula and other Vampires** was a stunning metaphor for dictatorships in Latin America; how power and death devour freedom and life. The scene with the group of virgins, students who are Dracula's fan club, makes this very clear. A group of tall men with vaporous tunics and militaristic vampire cloaks sucked dry and violated these innocent girls. These vampires are the germs of Nazism from old Europe, exported to Latin America. They develop and thrive in the innocent youth of a fertile land."

DRACULA AND OTHER VAMPIRES
Teatro Anchieta, São Paulo,
Brazil, 1995
Conceived and directed by
Antunes Filho

1 Production photo: Act I
2 Storyboard: Act I
3 Storyboard: Act I
4 Storyboard: Act I
5 Storyboard: Act I
6 Production photo: Act I
(following page)

AS ESTUDANTES DO INSTITUTO PANNICULUS V
GINALIS, SIMPATIZANTES DA VAMPIROMANIA E FU
DADORAS DE UMA ASSOCIAÇÃO NEO-VAMPÍRICA,
SITAM A TUMBA ONDE O ENIGMÁTICO CONDE D
CANSA. NA OCASIÃO, SÃO RECEBIDAS POR SU
GENERALA. DRÁCULA ERGUE-SE DE SEU TÚMULO E, H
NOTICAMENTE, SUBJUGA UMA DAS JOVENS.

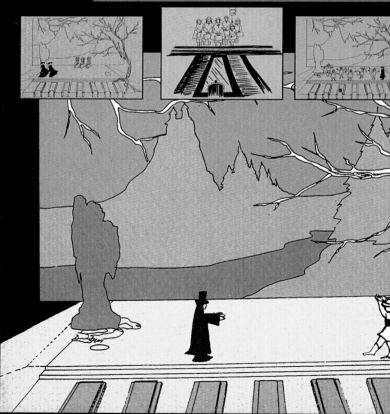

OS MENINOS, AGORA USANDO ASSOMBROSAS MÁSCARAS, VOLTAM AO CEMITÉRIO PARA EXORCIZAR OS ESPÍRITOS DOS VAMPIROS. DEPOIS DE PRONUNCIAR ALGUNS ESCONJUROS, OS JOVENS ACREDITAM EUFORICAMENTE NO ÊXITO DA EMPREITADA. É QUANDO, INESPERADAMENTE, RESSURGEM OS MORTOS-VIVOS.

UUUUU! UUUU! UUU! UUUUUU! UUUU! UUU! UUUU! UUUU! UUU!!!

UUUU!

DESEMBARCAM OS BELA LUGOSI DO MUSEU DE CERA DE DRÁCULA

A JOVEM SUGADA, AGORA UMA SONÂMBULA, IMERSA NO VÍCIO ABISSAL QUE DRÁCULA LHE INOCULARA, EM ÊXTASE AGÔNICO ENTREGA-SE A ELE MAIS UMA VEZ, NUMA OUSADA INVESTIDA, SEUS AMIGOS RETIRAM-NA DOS BRAÇOS DO CONDE. AS CORTESÃS PARTEM COM FÚRIA EM PERSEGUIÇÃO AOS JOVENS.

3

4

5

I do not passively adopt the actors' intentions or even the director's scene sketch. This has to be my point of departure from which I have to evolve ideas, work on them and return them strengthened. Sometimes in this process I transform them and return them as something else. There is never in my work an imposition stemming from vanity. I think that creative autonomy and vanity are better suited to the individuality of a plastic artist, a poet, a writer or a sculptor. This is not what I chose. Scenography is an integrated art: the more we listen and are listened to, the better the result will be, as you can see with **Zero**.

The text for the dance work **Zero** dealt with urban chaos in large metropolitan cities, São Paulo in this case. It all took place in the world of underground characters, in the chaos that large cities have with their insoluble problems of housing, social differences, unemployment, prostitution and disorderly growth. Talking to the German director – who was stunned by so many problems, even the issue of survival – we opted to create a space that would translate this chaotic architecture.

Coincidentally, during one of the director's visits to Brazil, a flyover was being inaugurated in Rio de Janeiro, one of those raised roads that are designed almost to invade buildings and houses. A photo showing the inauguration of the flyover presented the mayor of the city on this flyover, greeting a citizen who was inside his home and looking out by his window. Hans Kresnik, the director, was impressed by this invasion. The space of the play was there: public highways and bridges going through people's homes. We ripped the stage open, everything was on show, it was chaos. Inside that we built roads, some flyovers, painted with asphalt and with highway markings. We had many corners in the scenography. In one of them there was a huge pile of garbage with a plate that read: 'It is forbidden to steal garbage'. The show was very critical, irreverent and offered social denunciation through images. I deviated slightly from my visual 'aesthetic standard' in this production to attend to the various requests from the director. A synthesis was impossible. I had to be descriptive, in order to tell clearly a story that could not be told by the text.

Unfortunately we still improvise a lot in Brazil. Or fortunately, perhaps, I'm not sure. There are cases where improvisation, a last-minute solution, or a technical flaw, end up stimulating the designer to find another solution which is sometimes imaginative and makes the scene 'grow'. On the other hand, this business of the Brazilian way out of problems, what we call a 'flexible waist', gets on my nerves a little. I struggle for evolution in Brazil: of our theatre buildings; of our technical conditions; for an improvement in our métier; a greater awareness of the scenographer's craft etc. We need to progress. We need better conditions. We need more planning, too. But even if all that evolves a lot, there will always be room for improvisation. This is part of our culture and of our theatre as well.

JC SERRONI

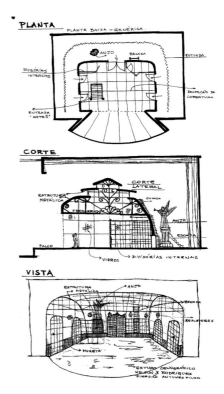

1

2

North Side Paradise is set amongst the families who live in the North Side, the poorest district of Rio de Janeiro. Serroni's sophisticated art nouveau set frames the dances, rituals and experiences of the grim lives of the characters in this fast-moving, internationally successful production. The set appeared to be realistic but it served the play in a very open manner and allowed for numerous different readings.

NORTH SIDE PARADISE
Adapted from plays by Nelson Rodrigues
Teatro Anchieta, São Paulo, Brazil, 1988
Directed by Antunes Filho

1 Sketches: Concepts and ideas for the production
2 Photograph: The basic set

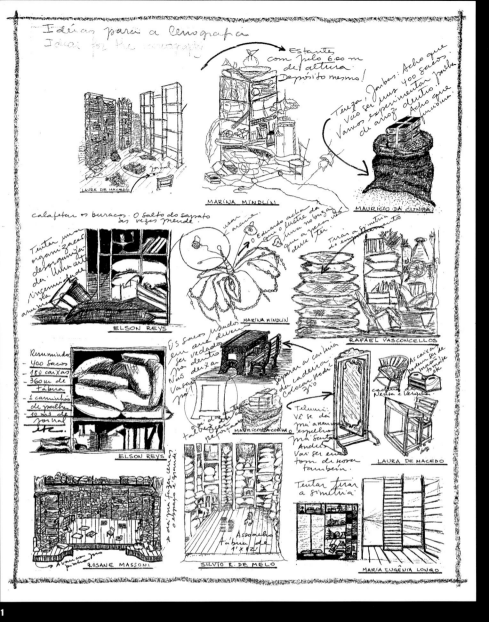

1

2

3

THE COFFEE TRADE FOXES
By Antonio Bivar and Celso
Luis Paulini
Tapa Group, Teatro Aliança
Francesa, São Paulo, Brazil, 1990
Directed by Eduardo Tolentino

1 Sketches: Concepts and ideas
for the production
2 Photograph: The basic set
3 Production photo: The basic set

The Coffee Trade Foxes was based on a 1922 event in São
Paulo during The Week of Modern Art. The text suggested that
the week was sponsored by the coffee barons, who travelled to
Europe and bought art objects, clothes and all sorts of bric-a-brac
which they kept in their coffee warehouses. "We used about 500
coffee sacks, filled with straw and newspaper, piled up on large
shelves. Those shelves surrounded the stage, creating a container
for the stage floor, which was free and always occupied by moving
things. The shelves were a kind of large prop table for the play's
furniture and objects. At times, actors, in character, were also on
the shelves and came out of them. It was as if this 'contour'
around the stage was a large book, which had characters
coming out of it to tell a story."

"The Western style of creation has had a tremendous impact; it creates new themes and forms of expression and enables me to develop a completely new kind of creativity."

YUKIO HORIO

Yukio Horio grew up in Hiroshima and studied stage design at Musashino Art University. In 1969, inspired by Western theatre practice, he went to study in Berlin. During the first ten years of his work subsequently in Japan he made stage props and special effects for the cinema, then his experience in the West began to appear in his design and he rose in prominence. Yukio Horio is a busy designer and runs a theatre-set manufacturing company. His monumental set for Yukio Ninagawa's production of **King Lear** is one of many that have attracted international attention. It followed a successful career of collaboration with many different artists, including Japanese stars such as Miyuki Nakajima and Hideki Noda. Inescapably influenced by traditional Japanese arts and yet deeply ambivalent about their utility for a contemporary scenographer, Yukio Horio displays the culturally nomadic versatility of an artist who is alive to the world's influences and whose career is marked by cross-cultural investigation and experiment.

INTERVIEW: I was an active member of the drama group in my junior and senior high schools and loved to perform in front of people. But I loved visual art more and used to go out to sketch the scenery in Hiroshima almost every week. I was vaguely thinking of becoming an artist at this time. When I had to choose my university, I gave up a career as an actor as I thought I had no talent for it – a career in theatre looked more fun than that of a lonely artist. So when I found a stage design course, I jumped at it. At that time it was the only course in Japan that specialised in stage design.

I don't have Japanese 'tradition' in me. For me, tradition is just a subject that I study or a useful resource for expressive technique which I occasionally use. I only use Japanese tradition with a Western interpretation; I never use it as it is because I am a free creator. I think this anecdote will explain what tradition is in Japanese art – it explains why I don't get involved.

The other day I heard that Miyuki Nakajima asked one of the traditional Noh Theatre actors if he was interested in performing with her. Ms Nakajima is a singer/artist whose annual show **Yakai** has been presented for a decade; it is very popular and the tickets can sell at a premium. She does everything – writing, composing, producing, performing and so on – sometimes with one or two co-performers. She had been thinking for some time of introducing Noh structure into one of her shows. In Noh Theatre at first the whole situation is presented to the audience by narration. When the narration comes to the important part, the Noh actor enlarges that part and plays. He dances, too, along with a chant and the orchestra joins in. She wanted that structure.

Knowing the popularity of her show, the Noh actor accepted the invitation. While discussing the production with him, Ms Nakajima said to the Noh actor, 'My show lasts for two months. Can you spend that long with me?' He replied, 'No problem. Even if I myself can perform for only three days, there are plenty of auxiliaries. All of them can do the same.' That is what a traditional art is. You cannot call it a traditional art if the art changes with the performer.

Perhaps this can be a form of theatre? Yet, in the world of Japanese and other Asian traditional arts, including Kabuki, children of three or four years old are forced by their parents to learn Kata or 'forms'. Sometimes, when they are older, they go to another school of the same tradition to learn, which means they copy this new house style; this is called 'mastering the art'. I tend to deny Japanese styles but recently I have had to admit that I naturally have a sense for the 'Japanese'. It's a fact that when the Japanese and Asian style of creation meets the Western style of creation this makes a 'big bang', and creates new themes and expression and this gives me completely new creativity.

Going to Berlin in 1969 was the natural extension of my yearning for the West. At that time, although 50 years had passed since Japan started to import the Western theatre of Ibsen and Chekhov, there was not much information available

2/2
Written and directed by Miyuki Nakajima
Bunkamara Theatre, Tokyo, Japan, 1997

1 Production photo: Scene played in a cheap hotel in Hanoi
2 Production photo: The final scene showing the sparkling Mekong river under the stage
3 Production photo: The opening scene of the show

2/2 was arranged and scripted from her own songs by the Japanese performer Miyuki Nakajima, well-known in Japan for her annual one-woman Evening Shows. As it was a solo show Horio was free to create an idiosyncratic staging. For the design concept he drew his metaphor from the dual personality and mental state of the character played by Nakajima and, for inspiration, he looked to the paintings of Francis Bacon: "Nakajima felt that the room was a cage and that the boat was freedom but that the mental state was the same, so I used Bacon's straight, black lines to represent the similarity." The process posed challenges as details from Nakajima were prone to sudden changes; after one meeting Horio left with the information that he had to include the entire Mekong river. These highly produced Evening Shows would be given up to 12 weeks to produce, unusual in Japan.

about the West. So when I first saw a book on stage art in Berlin, I was thrilled to realise that I was looking at what I had been yearning for. I was overwhelmed by the feeling. I thought, 'This is it; this is the theatre in the West!' The feeling reminded me of my childhood memory of seeing a porn magazine for the first time, my legs shaking as I looked at it. Although I enthusiastically studied Shakespeare, Goethe and Brecht, those two years in Berlin were a halfway measure. I didn't reach the essence of the West but, at the same time, I didn't accept my own country's tradition either. I revisited Berlin three years later but when my tutor, Professor Willi Schmidt, retired I returned to Japan. For the next ten years I worked around the world of theatre, making stage props and special effect props for films. But the influence of my experience in the West didn't appear until later.

Western audiences sometimes regard Japanese style a little suspiciously. When I was working on **Romeo and Juliet** the director Yukio Ninagawa at first wanted the streets of Italy – he is originally a realist. I persuaded him instead to use a series of grid-like frames which created three black corridors which suggested the Montagues' and Capulets' different culture and position. It also enabled us to focus on the speed of young people: for example, for the famous balcony scene, Romeo came from downstage to upstage centre and climbed up the frames like a monkey, not afraid of the height, to Juliet's window. These frames were also designed to hold about 20 secret doors. One night a buyer came from London, so Japanese producers and directors tried to impress him but he didn't 'bite': he felt that these frames of mine were 'well-made' but not 'ethnic' enough. Apparently Japanese well-made theatre was not good enough to take abroad! A year later, in 1999, Mr Ninagawa and I took an obviously 'Japanese' production of Shakespeare's **King Lear** to the Royal Shakespeare Company in London.

Taking a traditional Japanese play to Western audiences is also interesting. Some years ago we took the Kabuki story of **Oguri and Terute** to the Edinburgh Festival. The story was created when society believed more in the spiritual than the scientific. At that time, when people were beset by leprosy and disease, they could only pray. People were living in harmony with the spirits of the trees and the plants and also with the animals. To represent this atmosphere, I put two chickens on the stage which were eating round the actors' feet and clucking, fighting with the actors' concentration. The audience laughed a lot about this strange old Japanese story. Because it was not a modern play we could share the feeling of having the original human experience. If it had been a modern play the audience would not have been able to laugh and understand the point of the play because of the differences in culture and manner. I tried to make the audience 'feel the set' rather than 'read the set'. This was also the reason for the chickens.

As for my work process, if I think colour is the point when I read the script, I make a rough sketch using colour. When the focal point is the actor's movement, I start from a ground plan. The important thing is to grasp where the direction will

When Yukio Ninagawa first discussed his ideas for **Romeo and Juliet** with Horio he was keen to stage the play as an Italian Renaissance setting in the streets of Italy, as shown in Horio's original sketch for the production (1). Horio wanted to pursue a more metaphoric solution, and suggested a series of frames behind which there would be three black corridors that could indicate the culture and position of the two feuding families. The frames were all climbable and contained 20 secret doors.

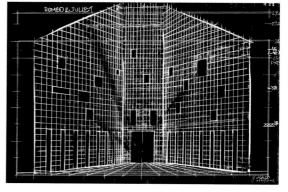

1

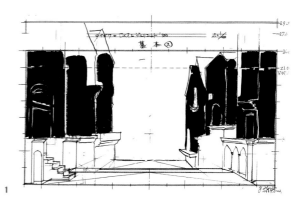

2

ROMEO AND JULIET
By William Shakespeare
Saitama Arts Theatre, Tokyo,
Japan, 1998
Directed by Yukio Ninagawa

1 Sketch: Original idea for the set based on a traditional Italian Renaissance setting
2 Sketch: Final idea for the set composed of frames
3 Production photo: Act I, Scene 1
4 Production photo: Act II, Scene 2
5 Production photo: Act V, Scene 3

Romeo and Juliet was Yukio Horio's first commission from Yukio Ninigawa; it was soon followed by Richard III, which they had to create by adapting the structure of the Romeo and Juliet set, as most of the money had been spent on that. It is particularly interesting to see a designer successfully create two contrasting settings from the same basic materials. The sculptural importance of white light is powerfully demonstrated in Richard III.

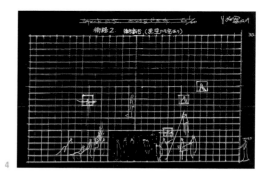

RICHARD III
By William Shakespeare
Saitama Arts Theatre, Tokyo,
Japan, 1998
Directed by Yukio Ninagawa

1 Production photo: Act I, Scene 3.
The palace
2 Production photo: Act II, Scene 1.
The palace
3 Production photo: Act II. Scene 3.
The street
4 Sketch: Act I
5 Sketch: Act II
6 Production photo: Act V, Scene 3,
Bosworth field
7 Production photo: Act V, Scene 5,
The battlefield

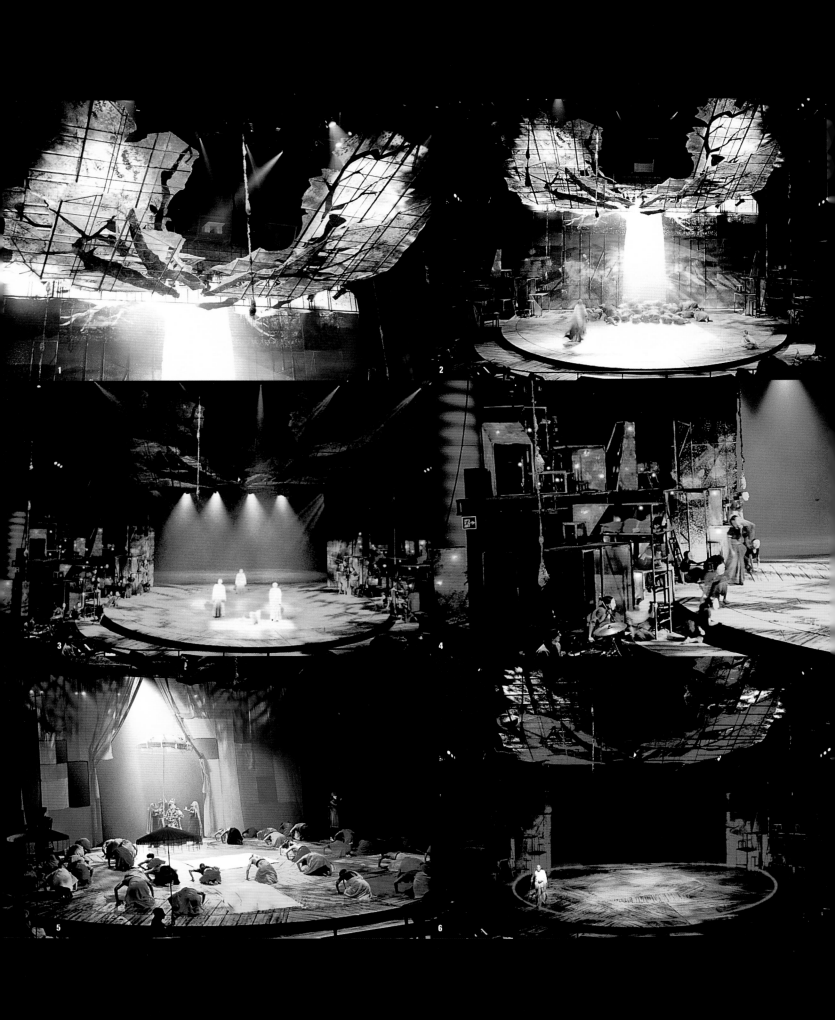

The story of **Buddha** preaching his sermon beneath a large linden tree is well known to Japanese audiences. Horio used smoke and inventive lighting to feature the tree's silhouette above the stage (1, 2). Horio's primary concern was with the staging of the epic with the intimate. His solution was to set the epic at the back of the stage and use lighting once again to isolate the intimate scenes downstage (3). He explains: "Part of the epic story is explaining people's impoverished lives, so I placed small lightbulbs in each of the 20 huts (4), which suggested a number of different vistas: people in India, a large city and even stars." Colour was also to feature strongly in telling the narrative. Horio chose yellow to represent Buddha, as he felt it to be a powerful way of representing India. He then developed this to combine with a red, neon light to represent Buddha's journey (5). "This was a breakthrough. The director then suggested the use of more colourful sets for the Indian palace and market." (6)

BUDDHA
By Osame Tezuka and Shinobu Sato
New National Theatre, Tokyo, Japan, 1998
Directed by Tamiya Kuriyama

1 Production photo: The leaves of the linden tree, made out of plastic
2 Production photo: Scene 1, Buddha gives a sermon to the people
3 Production photo: Scene 3, The tree has become the river Ganges and the story of Buddhism begins
4 Production photo: Scene 4, The 20 lit peasant huts by the river
5 Production photo: Scene 6, The crowd in the castle
6 Production photo: Scene 8, Buddha in contemplation during his travels

be focused and hold the design to that. If the script and direction emphasise the beauty of form, the starting point will be an elevation. If it is monumental, I immediately start from modelling. I often use models to explain and persuade. If necessary, I will use 1:10 scale or even life-size models. At my theatre-set manufacturing company I have the factory and people at my disposal for model-making. Directors and actors understand my ideas better if they can look at a model rather than at two-dimensional designs. It is important to talk the show through with a director at the earliest stage, using very rough sketches, almost scribbles. It should be left like that so that the image can grow and any change in the direction can be dealt with easily. Since this is a job in which you have to work with a director, the decisive factor is whether the two of you will get along. This is the reason why a new relationship is difficult to form and why you tend to repeat the same partnerships. I get excited when I see the synergy of the two creative forces, that of the director and that of the scenographer.

At the moment I am making great use of white light and the light curtain, mainly because it is in fashion and it's popular with Japanese directors and lighting designers. A stage designer who uses a model can't demonstrate a fade. He composes a clear space but, it is only when it comes to staging the model that the stage becomes a space available for lighting, as it is for a concert. The Czech scenographer Josef Svoboda and others have been doing this for 40 years or so but, in Japan, this type of expression has been developing over the last 15 years. The trend is gathering force with the constant development of mobile lighting systems. Even straight plays now adopt these mobile lighting systems.

One of the creative techniques of stage space is the 'air-perspective' method. This is used on top of the ordinary perspective to express depth by layers of air. For example, things near to you can look clear but things further away look fuzzy. Traditionally, a lot of backdrops are used. You can make pictures using backdrops but moving in and out of the picture is impossible. Smoke machines and new types of lighting equipment help solve this problem and create a feeling of depth. Of course, whether these things actually improve the quality of the production, is a different matter.

My motto is 'imagination surpasses theory' but ideas don't always come easily. Since I want to maintain certain professional standards, I have constructed my own theory. Yet I also feel that stage art should be free from any constraint. It should be expressed as you like, as it comes. Imagination should be free and there is no need for a theory. Why I quote my motto, when even I think it is exaggerated, is because I want to use it as a warning to myself. Art can become suffocated by theory. So I give imagination a priority. I rarely just come up with a design; it is more appropriate to say that I nurture a design. So I think I will change my motto to 'imagination leads theory'.

Kiru, meaning 'wear', is the story of love and war within the fashion industry in Mongolia. Horio responded by using many materials in the design including cotton, silk and wool. "**Kiru** is difficult for those who like Ibsen or Chekhov because it is a very physical play. When I design for Hideki Noda I try to make the set simple and to leave a clear space. He does not need darkness; **Kiru** offers a bright illusion." **Kiru** is related to Kabuki and to Noh. Acrobatics form a part of traditional Japanese theatre skills and are also performed in bright light. Bright light has been quite a dominant convention of Japanese performance; 30 years ago, German opera productions shocked Japanese audiences with their use of light and darkness: "We had never seen the art of darkness before. After that, we wanted to use that darkness and, in order to achieve this, theatre sets became darker too. I use a lot of darkness in my work, except when I design for Hideki Noda. The show and the set have to be real but also abstract and theatrical."

KIRU
Written and directed by
Hideki Noda
Osaka Kintetsu Theatre, Osaka,
Japan, 1997

1 Production photo: The son
follows in his father's foorsteps
2 Production photo: The son falls
in love after seeing a long love
letter written on the great wall
3 Production photo: China,
represented by silk
4 Production photo: Europe,
represented by wool

4

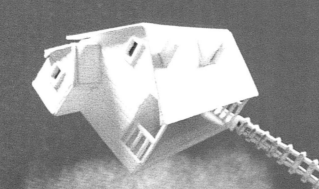

"**What I love**
about the theatre is its
theatricality
and the fact that you're
not reproducing real life on stage –
it's something more than that."

RICHARD HUDSON

After spending a childhood in the bush in Zimbabwe, Richard Hudson encountered stage design as a young student in England. He attended Wimbledon School of Art and became an assistant to the designers Nicholas Georgiadis and Yolanda Sonnabend for five years. Hudson distils visual source material into idiosyncratic and apt visions such as the gigantism of objects in **Into the Woods**; the extreme interior and exterior perspectives of **Lucia di Lammermoor** and **Oklahoma!** and the dynamic presentation of coloured and painted surfaces in **Samson et Dalila**. There is a confidence and clarity about Richard Hudson's designs that is reminiscent of the work of those artists who boldly evoke dreams. Richard's sense of narrative theatricality leads him to create settings that transform as a performance unfolds. As an Olivier and Tony award-winning designer, perhaps best known for his designs from the musical stage play **The Lion King** ©1997 Disney Enterprises, Inc., Richard Hudson straddles the mainstream and the avant garde. Underscoring the radicalism of Hudson's work is a respect for apprenticeship, for the past and for learning traditional drawing, drafting and model-making skills.

INTERVIEW: Some directors have very clear ideas about a production's atmosphere and visual world. Others are more intellectual and text-bound so a designer can be very influential about the visual style of the production. I like both. Opera directors tend to be a bit more adventurous and willing to take risks than theatre directors. I think there's a nervousness about the risk of the set or the look of a show taking over a play, which I understand. My job is to illuminate the play, not obscure it. At the same time, I'm not interested in designing a drawing-room comedy with French windows at the back. If I were, I would do television or perhaps film designing. What I love about the theatre is its theatricality and the fact that you're not reproducing real life on stage – it's something more than that.

In my experience, it's a disaster to insist on a concept if the director is not fully behind you. Theatre is a collaborative art and you have to work as a team with the director, lighting designer and costume designer – and all of you have to believe in the concept, otherwise it won't work. I like working with new people but I wouldn't want to work with a different director on every single project. The good thing about developing a relationship with a director is that you develop a kind of shorthand – you know instinctively what a director means and vice versa.

Work on a production tends to start a long way ahead. With opera, for example, you often start working one or two years before the production opens. I draw to begin with but, once I've got the model box built, I start working in that. Often I have ideas for sets just by putting bent bits of cardboard or some coloured paper in the box rather than trying to sketch something in a notebook. Directors prefer working with a model box too because they get a more immediate sense of the space. Some designers don't make models at all. In Italy, for example, many designers do the most exquisite renderings of what the set is going to look like, but they don't actually make a model of it. That way of working would make me terribly nervous because you don't get a sense of space or the relationship between the figure and the set.

I research each project, usually in a rather mundane way to begin with. In the case of **The Master Builder**, I looked at pictures of other productions of the play because I'd never seen it. I looked at pictures of Ibsen and his family and at pictures of objects and fashions of the time. Maybe I didn't use any of this but it was in my head when I was choosing. I suppose I used this research in the sense that the colours that I arrived at were probably informed by it. I can't always pinpoint it afterwards. My inspiration is more geometric than architectural. I use quite simple shapes that carve up the space. I like a slightly raked floor with an enveloping wall or cyclorama around it – used, for example, in the production of **Oklahoma!** I also like false perspective. I would only arrive at the decision to use a specific shape on stage after having tried many things in the model box.

1

OKLAHOMA!
By Richard Rodgers and
Oscar Hammerstein
UK tour, 1994
Directed by Christopher Renshaw

1 Research material: Photograph
by Walker Evans, 1936
2 Model: Act II, Scene 3, The
Barn
3 Model: Act II, Scene 1, Outside
the ranch house
4 Model: Act II, Scene 4
5 Model: Act II, Scene 5, Finale

2

3

4

5

Oklahoma! is a design which invokes the clear skies and epic scale of the American Midwest and the iconography of *The Wizard of Oz*. Hudson's design has a sharp-edged clarity, anchored around a palette of distinctive red, blue and yellow hues. "I feel that what I put on stage has to illuminate the play, opera or whatever, otherwise there is no point in doing it. I don't believe in obscuring something just to be provocative." This leads to a Magritte-like solidity to the idiosyncratic choices that he makes in some of his work. Hudson wanted his design to increase the virtual and actual space to give a palpable sense of the American open West, as well as allow enough space for the dancers: "There was a semi-circular floor that raked or could go flat for the dancing. Each act started with something miniature at the back and something linking it to the image at the front." During his research period Hudson collected images of American wooden architecture (1).

GUILLAUME TELL
By Giacomo Rossini, Etienne de
Jouy and Hippolyte Bis
Vienna State Opera, Vienna,
Austria, 1998
Directed by David Pountney

1 Model: Act I, Scene 1
2 Production photo: Act IV. Scene 2.
Finale
3 Model: Front cloth
4 Model: Act II, Hunter's chorus

1

2

3

4

With **Guillaume Tell** (William Tell) Hudson's enquiry into the meaning of the opera leads to the inspirations of Romantic painting, of rural crafts and architecture of the Alpine landscape, but also to the cruelty and politics of the opera. "I suppose that little wooden houses are a recurrent theme in my work. In **Guillaume Tell** I did little Swiss houses (1). I bled a gauze into this carved Swiss landscape. " The chorus of Austrian huntsmen (4) was rowdily booed by the Viennese audience when the production was first performed: "They had helmets with antlers on and wore military-style costumes. Yet in the story the Austrians are horribly cruel to the Swiss."

I think my work is changing now in that it is getting more symbolic or painterly, not so literal. A lot of my research material is quite abstract. I often tear out pages from magazines which feature an image or colour or texture which serves as a starting point. For **Samson et Dalila** (Samson and Delilah) I collected images featuring the hot colours I was trying to emulate. To some extent I was trying to reach a similar painterly feel to the works of Matisse or Howard Hodgkin with their strong colours and bold strokes. This kind of painting is often so difficult to reproduce on stage. When I made the model I used my fingers to paint the patterns on the cloth by dipping them into a tray of black paint. However, the real back cloth at the Met is absolutely vast but the set painters managed to paint it beautifully and with a feeling of spontaneity.

The Americans call my style 'whimsical', although I would prefer to use the word 'quirky'. I was thrilled and surprised to be asked to do **The Lion King** for Broadway, particularly because it was set in Africa where I had lived for 18 years. The project was also very appealing when it was made clear to me that the management definitely didn't want it to look like the movie – I'd never even seen the animated film; I had to go out and buy a video. I think when Disney did **Beauty and the Beast** for the stage they came in for a lot of criticism – people in the theatre were saying 'why are you reproducing your films on stage?' No doubt this is one reason why I was asked to do the set. **The Lion King** was fairly stressful to work on but I'm sure the audience have no idea how half the scenery gets there and I'm glad they don't. The mechanics, the hydraulics and the computers off-stage are unbelievable, but are not necessarily apparent on stage.

It is vital for a designer to think about the set changes and the way a set is revealed and taken away from an audience. For example, the set changes for **Eugene Onegin** at Glyndebourne were also part of the design solution. The opera is episodic – Tchaikovsky sub-titled it 'Pages from the Life of Eugene Onegin', so I wanted to solve this problem to begin with. I settled on a stylistically simple Russian/Shaker feel for the set with gauze curtains on tracks at the front and at the back. At the start the audience vaguely saw the image of the mother and Tatiana's sister through the gauze. Then a curtain swept across very slowly as the chorus came on. At the end of the scene the gauze came back again. Meanwhile the curtain at the other end of the box was going the other way; it was as though the image was being wiped out very slowly. While it was travelling across, they did a very quick set change, so that by the time the curtains had gone, we were in Tatiana's bedroom. For Stravinsky's **The Rake's Progress** in Chicago, all the scenes changed in

Samson et Dalila (Samson and Delilah) was an opera which Hudson redesigned twice before it was approved by the director. "The second time I designed it I was told it bore some resemblance to something already in the repertoire. This one, the third one, was best. The director wanted it to have an African feel, so I took North Africa as my influence." Hudson's painstaking research includes pages torn from magazines of anything that featured strong, hot colours (1). He also collected images of explosions (2) for the final scene as well as reproductions from numerous painters, in particular Franz Kline (8). Matisse was also a strong influence for the nude figure on the front cloth (3), as well as for many of the colours and shapes (5). Act II, Scene 2 (4) featured an explosive black back-cloth: "I painted that cloth on the model with my fingers, dipped in a plate of black paint." The inspiration for Act II, Scene 1 (7) was taken from a drawing he found of tall North African mud houses with spikes (9). "The spiky shapes were on the gauze so that they looked like they were floating. They started off very high and during the act they floated down so they appeared to be entrapping Samson."

SAMSON ET DALILA
By Camille Saint-Saëns and
Ferdinand Lemaire
Metropolitan Opera House,
New York, USA, 1998
Directed by Elijah Moshinsky

1 Research material: Influence for
desert colours
2 Research material: Influence for
the collapse of the temple
3 Model: Front cloth to Act II
4 Model: Act I, Scene 2, Chorus
of The Old Hebrews
5 Model: Act I, Scene 6, Dance of
the Priestesses of Dagon
6 Model: Act III, Scene 2, The
Bacchanale
7 Model: Act II, Scene 1, Outside
Dalila's house
8 Research material: *Ballantine*,
1948–60, Franz Kline
9 Research material: Hudson
found this image of North African
huts which influenced the
structures in Act II, Scene 1

9

7

Hudson says that this production of Verdi's **Lucia di Lammermoor** comes from the forced perspective phase he went through, also to be seen in his designs for Ostrovsky's **Too Clever By Half** at the Old Vic Theatre in London, 1988. The tunnel effect grew deeper and deeper as the opera progressed. After Zurich he was able to extend the design in Munich, which has a much deeper stage. In the 'mad' scene at the end he could make the portals at the back move, so that the perspective became distorted as Lucia moved like a tightrope walker towards the audience. This evocative, moving, expressionist approach, slightly reminiscent of Robert Wiene's early German film *The Cabinet of Dr Caligari* meant that the distorting staging could parallel, reflect and comment upon Lucia's derangement.

LUCIA DI LAMMERMOOR
By Gaetano Donizetti and
Salvatore Cammarano
Zurich Opera, Zurich,
Switzerland, 1989
Directed by Robert Carsen

1 Model: Act I, Scene 2
2 Model: Act II, Scene 4
3 Model: Act II, Scene 1
4 Research material: Coffered ceiling in Czechoslovakia

4

front of the audience. It was a very simple device, just borders and wings, all done by computer. Pink ones slid on in front of blue ones so it was like the iris of a camera; it just went vroom, pink, and at the end of that it went vroom, yellow. It was very startling.

Much of what happens on stage these days is computerised but this can be combined with much simpler methods which are sometimes more effective. For **Into the Woods** in the West End of London, Richard Jones was very keen that we didn't do a naturalistic wood. For months we tried different ways of presenting trees. Trees on stage are always a nightmare. It ended up as a cyclorama, like a Doré etching of trees from a Victorian child's illustrated book. Stephen Sondheim looked a bit perplexed when he first came to see the model. It was somewhat different from the New York production! At the end of the musical the giantess tried to get her revenge on Jack who has killed the giant. The door flew open and an enormous, swivelling eye appeared. The eye was three dimensional and was moved by the crew; it appeared to be looking through the hole. An enormous finger came through another door. At the very end, when the giantess gets killed, the proscenium arch fell down. A very simple device – just a piece of black cloth obscuring half the set – and then the giant's wife's huge spectacles fell onto the stage.

Lighting sometimes gets the short straw and yet it is terribly important. Good lighting design can make something rather dull look quite good or even wonderful on stage; it can also make something wonderful look ghastly. The colour, atmosphere, the texture, everything about the set is influenced by the lighting. Certainly I'm always there at lighting sessions. I might sit back and keep my mouth shut but if there is something I don't like, I will certainly say so.

One of the things I love about my profession is that it is achieved with different people, in different places and each project is different. I also love the fact that my job finishes on the first night. The audience sees it for the first time and they either clap or they boo. When it comes to the end of its run, the set's thrown out and that's that.

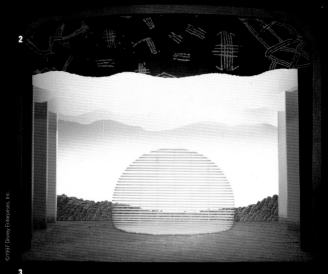

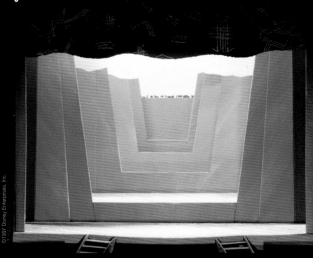

THE LION KING

Designs © 1997 Disney Enterprises, Inc.
"The Lion King"
Original Broadway Production, opened at the New Amsterdam Theatre,
November 13, 1997
Music and Lyrics by Elton John and Tim Rice
Book by Roger Allers and Irene Mecchi
Scenic Design Richard Hudson
Costume Design Julie Taymor
Lighting Design Donald Holder
Mask & Puppet Design Julie Taymor & Michael Curry
Sound Design Tony Meola
Hair & Makeup Design Michael Ward
Choreography by Garth Fagan
Directed by Julie Taymor

1 Model: The elephants' graveyard
2 Model: The sunrise
3 Model: The wildebeest stampede
4 Model: The jungle

1

2

3

4

Golden Cuckoo
instead of Clock

5

6

7

The musical **Into the Woods** combines some of the darker aspects of traditional fairytales. Hudson collected reference material that included clocks and moons as well as numerous illustrations from Victorian books (9–12). The many doors around the circular main room were designed to create a dreamlike effect of other-worldliness. Antlers were used in the backs of chairs (2–6). "In the second Act I wanted to show the wallpaper peeling and cracked and that the giant cuckoo clock at the back had fallen apart, exploded, with all its innards coming out (5, 6). At the end the giantess tries to get her revenge because the giant has been killed by Jack. The door flew open and this enormous swivelling eye, moved by the stage crew, appeared, as though she was looking through the hole." (5) When the giantess is killed Hudson used a simple but effective device of a piece of black to stage the collapsing proscenium arch (6).

Scene 2a

10

THE CLOCK
travelling through the set

11

cloth comes up through
the floor

"FIRST MIDNIGHT"

ACTORS PASS IN FRONT OF THE CLOTH WITH THE PROVERBS ON
BANNERS

Scene 3

JACK:
" THERE ARE GIANTS IN THE SKY"

12

INTO THE WOODS
By Stephen Sondheim and
James Lapine
Phoenix Theatre, London,
UK, 1990
Directed by Richard Jones

1 Model: Act I, Curtain
2 Model: Act I, The wedding
3 Model: Act I, Scene 3, "There
are giants in the sky"
4 Sketch: The cuckoo
5 Model: Act II, The woods
6 Model: Act II, Finale
7 Production photo: Act I,
The wedding
8 Storyboard: Act I, Scenes
2a and 3
9 Research material: Glasses
for the final scene
10 Research material: Victorian
illustration
11 Research material: Clock
in Prague
12 Research material: Influence
for peeling wallpaper

8

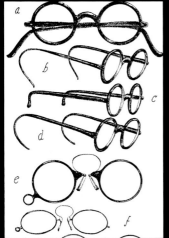

9

10

11

12

"**A designer's role is that of**

conceptual architect:

We create a framework upon which, and within which, many people, including ourselves,

can continue to have ideas."

THE SPIRIT OF '76

ADRIANNE LOBEL

Adrianne Lobel grew up in Brooklyn, New York. Her parents were both artists and loved the theatre, so when she was young, she was exposed to New York's museums and theatres. While in high school, she studied painting at The Brooklyn Museum School and then took classes in theatre design at a small studio school in Greenwich Village. When she was 18, Adrianne decided to go West to see what would happen. In Hollywood she obtained work as a 'set designer' or draftsperson, which provided an invaluable apprenticeship when, two years later, she returned to the East coast to study design with Ming Cho Lee at Yale. Adrianne Lobel has designed in American Regional Theatres, on and off Broadway and for opera, dance, music, videos and film. Her collaborations with director Peter Sellars include **The Mikado** (1983); **Cosi Fan Tutte** (1986) and **The Marriage of Figaro** (1990); **Nixon in China** (1987/2000) and Mozart's **The Magic Flute** (1990). Another longstanding relationship is with American choreographer Mark Morris and includes the productions **L'Allegro, il Penseroso ed il Moderato** (1988) and **Platée** (1997/2000). She has also worked frequently with directors James Lapine and Francesca Zambello.

INTERVIEW: The Hollywood experience was an invaluable advantage to me at Yale. Instead of learning to draft, I was able to struggle with design ideas. I could see my own work realised for the first time and, most importantly, I could enjoy and be stimulated by other designers, directors, playwrights and actors. I recommend working as an apprentice or an assistant in a professional situation but I don't recommend it in lieu of design school. Bob Brustein from Yale went to Harvard and established the American Repertory Theatre. He invited me to work with Peter Sellars, a young director whose undergraduate productions he had been impressed by. That was a world that kept opening. It led to Mark Morris and working in opera and in Europe.

When you start work, the rough sketching phase can last from three days to two weeks. It is an emotional roller coaster. The big idea always comes in an instant, even if you've been drawing for days. Sometimes it's just recognising what you've been drawing. Figuring out the big idea, that flash when you realise your drawing has led you to an approach, is the most gratifying moment in the course of a show. The idea will dictate the mode of development. Is it better to start making rough models or a series of collages or to continue to sketch in a more fine-tuned way? How best to show your idea to a director? If you have collaborated with the director before and she/he can read your sketches, you can show her/him the roughest of drafts. I don't like to show anything until I have some readable sketches of the big idea that has developed. Then I will show the voyage from the extreme roughs to the clearer ones – which are still very mushy.

After Peter Sellars and I had done Mozart's **Cosi Fan Tutti** set in a roadside diner by the sea and surrounded by 18th-century painted trees, he asked me to design Mozart's **The Marriage of Figaro**, also for the Pepsico Summerfare. This was the late 1980s, the height of the Reagan era when real estate was booming in Manhattan and Donald Trump was king. Peter and I knew that we wanted to set the show in New York but we were not sure if the super-rich Count and Countess were living in the Upper West Side in a big, pre-war apartment or perhaps in a townhouse on the Upper East Side.

I felt it was important to have a big sense of sky, like in a Fragonard painting. **The Marriage of Figaro** takes place in one day. I wanted to see the passage of time in the changes of the sky. I also wanted to have a sense of the high and low – the rich above, the poor on the city streets below. Through the sketching process, I discovered that the Count and Countess lived in Trump Tower, high above the streets in a penthouse that functions on a feudal system. They have a chauffeur – Figaro; a maid – Susanna; a florist and so on. Now that I had the idea, I needed to research. What did $3–5 million apartments look like? I dressed myself up, posed as a fancy interior decorator searching for a glamorous apartment for a celebrity client. Much to my surprise, the real estate agents believed me, showed me many multi-million dollar apartments and allowed me to take pictures!

1

Lobel describes **Lady in the Dark** as "the first mid-life crisis musical". In this show the actuality scenes are spoken and the dreams are the musical numbers: "Liza, the protagonist, falls asleep in her office chair or she tells a dream to her shrink and we are transported to musical dream/nightmare land. The melody that keeps beating in her head is 'My Ship has Sails' but Liza doesn't remember the words until her breakthrough at the end of the show. I drew triangular sails again and again...and then I looked at Feininger's paintings of geometric ships. I liked the idea that Liza's answer was right there in front of her, that she was wandering around lost in her own brain – the set – from which memories and dreams could come at her. The abstract sail shapes would be a tangible metaphor for her confusion and her release. Literally she is 'at sea'. I also liked that the sail shapes were graphic manifestations of rays of light."

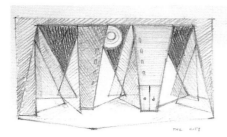

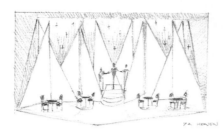

2

LADY IN THE DARK
By George Gershwin and
Kurt Weill
Royal National Theatre, London,
UK, 1997
Directed by Francesca Zambello

1 Research material: *Sailboats*,
1929, Lyonel Feininger. The
Detroit Institute of Arts, Detroit
2 Storyboard: Various scenes
3 Model: Second dream,
Graduation
4 Model: Final scene. Circus
5 Production photo: Second
dream, Graduation
6 Production photo: Final
scene, Circus

5

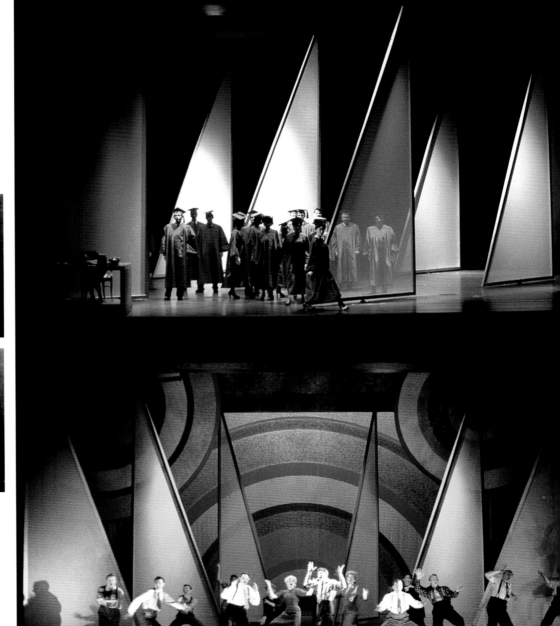

3

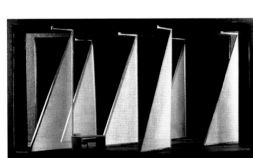

4

6

L'ALLEGRO, IL PENSEROSO ED IL MODERATO

By Frederick Handel and
John Milton
Théâtre de la Monnaie, Brussels,
Belgium, 1988
Directed and choreographed by
Mark Morris

1 Research material: *Homage to the Square – Joy*, 1964, Joseph Albers, James Goodman Gallery, New York

2 Research material: *Untitled*, 1951–5, Mark Rothko, Tate Gallery, London

3 Watercolour sketches: 'Come thou Goddess, fair and free'

4–7 Models: From some of the 150 transient scenes which made up this production

8–11 Watercolour sketches: Revealing Lobel's experimentation with colour and form

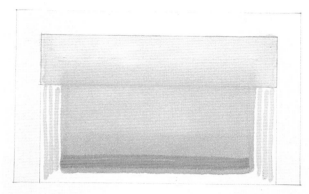

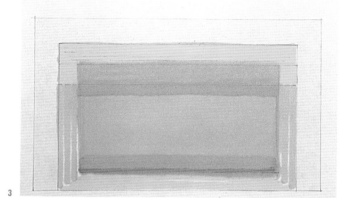

L'Allegro, il Penseroso ed il Moderato was one of Lobel's favourite productions to design. She chose an abstract route which allowed her to create a fluid and expressive environment and used the paintings of Mark Rothko and Josef Albers as her influences: "It became clear that the colour planes would be drops bordered by white portals that receded upstage in perspective like the borders in Albers. In this way you could see the edges of the pure colour of one drop against the portal both behind and in front of it. In the model I figured out the spacing of the portals and the amount I wanted them to perspect. Mostly I spent hours in my kitchen over steaming pots of boiling dye, dying organza different colours. I made dozens of coloured scrim drops out of organza and translucent drops made of different colour pantone paper. In this way I could see how one colour would affect another and work out how many drops and what colour I needed to create the landscapes I wanted. Aside from the geometric modernity of the set, it could have been a 19th-century ballet setting with portals and drops."

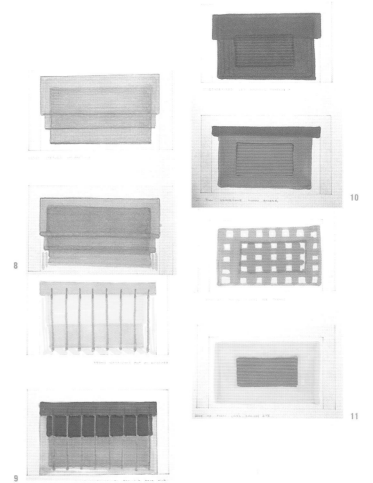

8

9

10

11

7

THE MARRIAGE OF FIGARO

By Wolfgang Amadeus Mozart
and Lorenzo Da Ponte
Pepsico Summerfare, Purchase,
New York, USA, 1990
Directed by Peter Sellars

1, 2 Research material: Lobel's
photographs of high-rise
apartments
3, 4 Research material: Lobel's
photographs of Trump Tower,
New York
5 Research material: *La Fête à
Saint Cloud*, Jean Fragonard,
Banque de France, Paris
6 Drawing: Trump Tower trees
7 Drawing: The basic set
8 Production photo: Interior
with trees
9 Production photo: The
basic set

Lobel found her big idea for **The Marriage of Figaro** by solving
the problem of the rooms posed by the libretto. Having decided
upon visiting upscale apartments, she had a mass of research
material (1, 2). She chose Trump Tower (3, 4) as her direct
inspiration for the resolution of Act IV: "Trump Tower has tiers
of dry-looking pine trees that cling in terror to a series of glass
steps on the corner of the building. I flew in another glass wall
downstage of the Act III duplex set so that we felt we were
looking at the exterior of the building and brought on a low
balcony with fake pine trees covered in little white twinkling
lights (8). This never failed to get a chuckle of recognition out
of New York audiences. With the smoked-glass walls, it was
like looking straight through the building from exterior to interior.
The changing sky, reflected in the glass via James F. Ingalls'
stunning lighting, captured a limpid, Fragonard-like feeling
for the 18th century (5) and was also totally modern."

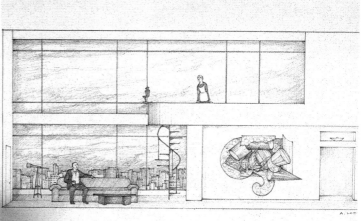

For **The Diary of Anne Frank** Lobel wanted to avoid the obvious but alternatives weren't working. "The director and I realised that it was valiant but foolish to resist the old-fashioned format of the play. There were going to be many school children coming to see this show. We wanted them to experience realistically the situation of eight people living in cramped quarters for three years." The major problem was that the annex the family lived in was on three levels. "Doing a three-level set on a stage, especially when the most intimate scenes take place at the highest level, is not a great idea because of the sightline problems that arise. The highest level, in order for anything to be seen, would have to be pushed so far upstage that the actors would be 30ft from the front row. Also the front few rows would get whiplash craning their necks to look up so high! I had to figure out a way to fit all the rooms of the annex within a two-story structure. I enjoy a puzzle of this kind. The problem has been posed. All that remains is to solve it. Posing this problem is by far the most difficult exercise."

THE DIARY OF ANNE FRANK
By Frances Goodrich and Albert Hackett and adapted by Wendy Kesselman
Music Box Theatre, New York, USA, 1997
Directed by James Lapine

1 Production photo: The basic set
2 Early model: The basic set
3 Model: The basic set

ON THE TOWN
By Betty Comden, Adolph
Green and Leonard Bernstein
New York Shakespeare Festival
Delacorte Theatre,
New York, USA, 1997
Directed by George C. Wolfe

1 Drawing: The bridge
2 Model: The bridge
3 Production photo: The bridge

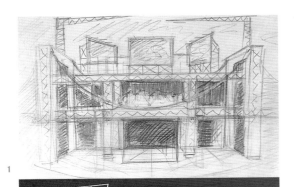

1

2

3

The narrative unfolds architecturally over one day. It begins with Figaro
measuring the room to see how his bed will best fit into the tiny space; Act II
is the Countess's bedroom; Act III is a great hall or a large living room and, in the
last Act, a pine forest is called for. Figaro and Susanna's room became a laundry
room complete with the requisite appliances and a convertible sofa that, when
opened, filled the entire width of the room and had to be clambered over to get
from one side to the other. The couch that we found had a life of its own and
would sometimes close up if stepped on in a certain spot. This led to staging
that was truly laugh-out-loud funny. This production was wildly controversial
and is one of Peter's and my best collaborations.

My favourite production and design was Mark Morris's full-length choreography
for Handel's 1740 **L'Allegro, il Penseroso ed il Moderato** based on a 1630s'
student poem by Milton. It is not a narrative, it's more of an argument as to the
different ways you can choose to live your life. L'Allegro – go out dancing and
drinking every night, be happy, giggle a lot, hunt the fox, have sex; Il Penseroso
– be meditative, quiet, spiritual, reap the rewards of solitary reflection; Il Moderato
– figure out a way to have a nice, happy medium.

Listening to the music, I heard that for every verse of poetry there were distinct
changes in tone. Handel had already accomplished his musical 'illustration' of the
verses. My job, it seemed, was to illustrate with scenery. I started to sketch. At
first I made some really literal choices. If sheep and clouds were mentioned, I
drew sheep and clouds. But soon I realised that this was not my job at all. We
heard the words, we didn't need to repeat the images that were written. I needed
to create a fluidly shifting and expressive environment in which the dancers could
move from thought to thought. I got rid of all specifics and began to work with
abstract planes of colour. In arranging and rearranging these colour planes, I
could create literal landscapes – of green fields and blue sky, of sunset and dawn,
of monasteries and cities – that were also non-literal landscapes – of joy, sorrow,
of peace, of excitement. I looked at Rothko's and Albers' paintings. I wanted to
present the emotional impact of colour, of a colour against a colour and the
changing composition of more of one colour and less of another.

The hard part was technical. This was the first time I'd ever dealt with a
computerised system. Some of the theatre's flies were manual, which means
someone had to fly in a drop on cue. About two-thirds of the fly lines were on
a computer which meant one person could push a button and 'on cue' three
drops could move at three different speeds and fly to three different trims. This
system made the creation of **L'Allegro, il Penseroso ed il Moderato** possible.
The set became a giant musical instrument, an organ that was capable of
accomplishing great, complicated chords. Designing these moves is what
occupied most of the tech time. I had drawn through the show but once I saw
the dance on stage I needed to make adjustments and to choreograph the set
around the choreography. The first run-through was a mess and I needed three
intense days to get things to work. If the drops moved at what seemed like a

NIXON IN CHINA
By John Adams and Alice Goodman
Houston Grand Opera, Houston,
USA, 1987
Directed by Peter Sellars

1, 2 Research material: Photographs
of Nixon's visit to Beijing Airport from
the Associated Press Office, USA
3 Model: Act I, The Welcome
Banquet
4 Model: Act I, The Welcome
Banquet
5 Drawing: Act I, Scene 1, Beijing
Airport
6 Production photo: Chairman
Mao's library
7 Drawing: Aria
8 Production photo: Conference
9 Production photo: Act I, Scene 3,
The Welcome Banquet

When Lobel began work on the premiere of the new opera **Nixon in China**, the piece had not been orchestrated. Lobel started with research as opposed to 'thought drawings', as the structure of the opera was quite prosaic, following the trip that Nixon made to China in 1972. "This event was mostly a giant, staged photo opportunity. The first scene is on the tarmac of Beijing airport; crowds of soldiers await the arrival of the President's plane, Air Force One. The plane arrives; this is one of the great musical crescendos for the arrival of a piece of scenery in the history of opera, thank you John! Nixon and Mao Tse Tung meet; they talk philosophy. Mao has the upper hand, Kissinger is in way over his head and the Chinese Premiere Chou en Lai keeps the peace."

"Act I, Scene 3 is The Welcome Banquet (9); a great many photographers recorded every second. In order to look at photographs of this trip, I called the Associated Press Office, conveniently located in the Time/Life building in the Rockefeller Centre; a research person obtained exactly what I needed within minutes. I chose about 30 images; these photographs became the inspiration for everyone involved with the production." (1, 2)

1

Lobel's biggest design concern with **Platée** was to provide large areas for dance and still create an organic-looking swamp. Her answer was to stage the Prologue in a New York bar which would disappear off-stage and become a terrarium, where the audience would be transported into a world of miniature scale: "Now the 'swamp' could be as artificial as a stage setting. There was a blown-up photo backing of a swamp (the kind you tape to the back of your terrarium to make your pet feel at home), a large artificial plant and a fake cave, a bright orange plastic water dish that could become a fountain and, best of all, a flat expanse of dance floor. Aside from the water dish I kept my palette in the dull greens and browns. This allowed Isaac Mizrahi to go insane with colour for his costumes."

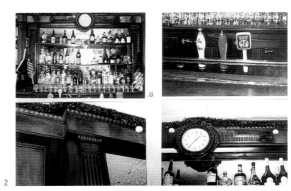

2

3

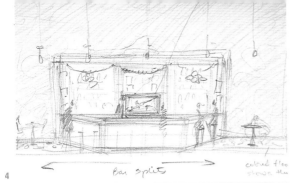

4

5

6

7

PLATÉE
By Jean Philippe Rameau
Royal Opera House, London,
UK, 1997
Directed by Mark Morris

1 Production photo: Prologue,
The New York bar
2 Research material: Lobel's
photographs of New York bars
3 Production photo: Act I, The
terrarium
4 Sketch: Prologue, The New
York bar
5 Model: Prologue, The New
York bar
6 Sketch: Act I, The terrarium
7 Model: Act I, The terrarium

musically appropriate speed and landed on a perfect note, they were invisible. We would work all day and the dancers would come on stage in the evening. These were three of the most intense and thrilling days of my life. The show was and is breathtaking, a classic in the Mark Morris canon and has played all over the world.

A designer's role is that of conceptual architect. We create a framework upon which and within which many people, including ourselves, can continue to have ideas. This is how you know if your big idea works and is a good big idea, if it seems to be opening up possibilities. There are rare occasions when the conceptual idea appears full grown in your mind without the sketching process. Take **Platée**, which was originally done as a court masque and was predominantly danced. It takes place in a swamp that is inhabited by Platée and her dominion, including bugs, snakes, turtles, butterflies, fish and satyrs. Platée is dying for a boyfriend. Her love life has not gone well – maybe it's because she's terribly ugly and slimy too. The story complicates and it all ends in terrible humiliation for poor, green Platée.

My biggest design concern was figuring out how to provide large areas for dance and still create an organic-looking swamp. I had flu and was between naps and beyond caring when, all of a sudden, I sat upright in bed. 'Oh, the Prologue takes place in an old New York bar, in front of the mirrored shelves with all the bottles on them. And the opera takes place in the terrarium!' I laughed and let my head fall back on the pillow. I don't think I'd even been thinking about the show. During the transition from the Prologue to Act I, the bar counter would split and be whisked off-stage by dancers, the bar wall with terrarium would fly (with the terrarium glowing) and we would find ourselves transported to miniature scale and into the world of Platée. A sort of 'Honey, I Shrunk the Drunks'.

Most of the time designers are hired too late. Only in the opera world are you given enough time to get to know a piece and then let ideas gestate over a couple of weeks before sitting down to work. I don't think my fever idea would have come to me if the show hadn't been in my head for some time. Most opera houses run in repertory – they present two or three different productions on their stage in a week with a 'change-over' of only a few hours. Your set has to fit in and around someone else's inevitably huge production of Verdi's **Aida**. This means you can't use all the fly lines – you only have a few to choose from. And there is a rigid electric hanging plot. Lights are refocused for each show but they are not rehung. So if you want your cloud to fly in right there, think again.

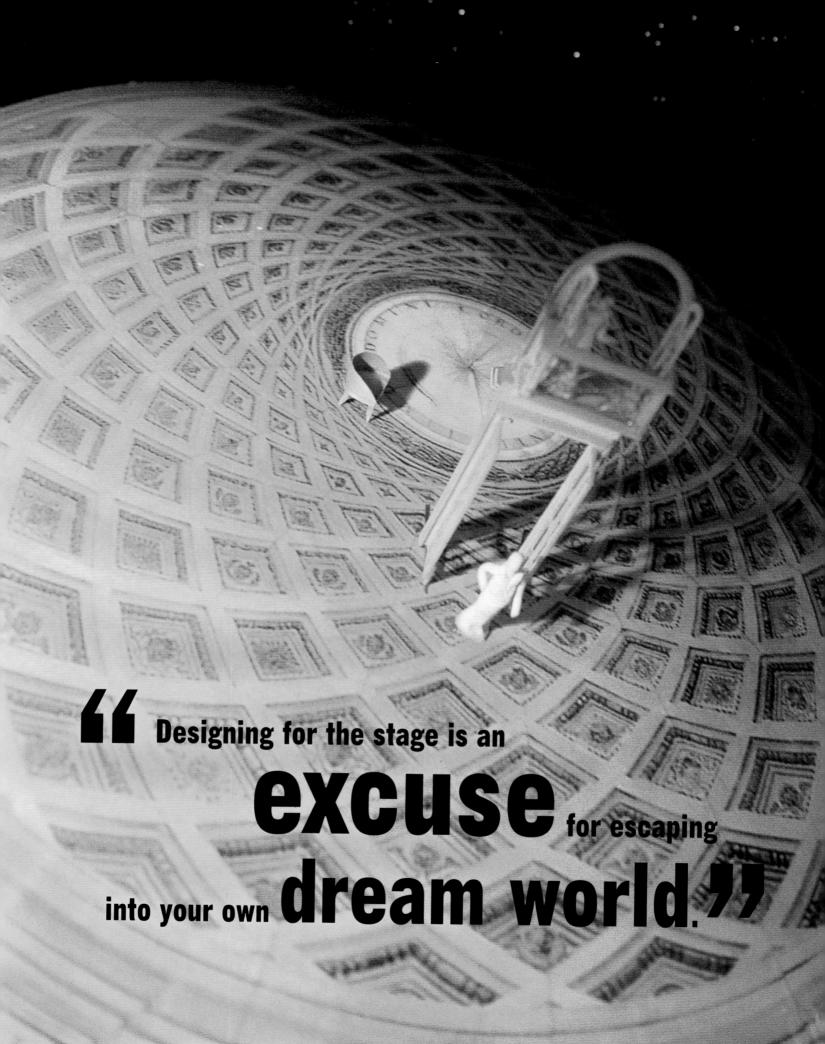

" Designing for the stage is an **excuse** for escaping into your own **dream world.** "

GEORGE
TSYPIN

George Tsypin graduated from Moscow Architectural Institute in 1977 and that same year became a winner of the 'New and Spontaneous Ideas for the Theatre of a New Generation' competition in Paris. Since 1979 he has lived and worked in America. After working for a year in the architectural firm HLW in New York, he became a graduate student of set design at New York University. Immediately after graduation in 1984, he was invited to design four shows at the newly formed American National Theatre at the Kennedy Centre in Washington. After designing numerous theatrical productions in almost all American theatres in the early 1990s, he launched an international career in opera. Tsypin also expanded his design work to include concerts, film and television productions, as well as exhibitions, interior design and installations. He has had a gallery show of his sculptures in New York and has received numerous awards. He has worked for many years with the director Peter Sellars, as well as with renowned directors Julie Taymor, Robert Falls, Jurgen Flimm and Andrey Konchalovsky. He has a special creative relationship with the conductor Valery Gergiev.

INTERVIEW: My early training as an architect remains a main impulse in my work. The sets I design seem too big for the stage, for the theatre, for the building itself. They have no boundaries, they seem to burst through the walls. They are in constant clash with the architecture that is supposed to enclose them. They are in the process of destruction and rebuilding at the same time, as if the design itself is an attempt to break through into another world. Whether working on **Saint Francis of Assisi**, **War and Peace** or Wagner, it usually comes down to finding a spiritual dimension of space. Today, when movies, television, computers – all flat projections on the screen – are dominating our visual world, theatre uniquely takes place in space. In theatre there is nothing more powerful than the space.

Designing for the stage is an excuse for escaping into your own dream world. Design for opera, in particular, frees you almost completely from the narrative and practicalities of the theatrical action. I see myself as the co-author of the whole event, along with the composer, director and conductor. You try to establish a direct connection to the music through other media: space; sculpture; movement and light. Everything starts with the sound and then the world is created on stage. During the first ten minutes of the **Ring Cycle** there is almost nothing but one note, E-flat, in total darkness. It is the beginning of the world. First we see a tiny light, the conductor's baton. Then the tiny lights, stars, multiply, and finally a powerful, blinding, single beam of light reveals the world of the stage. The music, the orchestra and the conductor become the life source, the heart of the show.

This original impulse became a guiding force for the **Ring Cycle**. The world exploded around the orchestra; some of the audience found themselves floating above the stage, and with elements of the set in the middle of the house, backstage, crushing against the walls, piercing the ceiling and the floor. The orchestra itself, as if loosing the anchor of the orchestra pit, appears either on stage or so far in the house that you can't distinguish between musicians and the audience. And the singers seem close, like a cinematic close-up and then they reappear 100ft away, in a long shot.

For a few months I was struggling with the concept, shuttling between New York and Amsterdam, taking enormous models back and forth. When you reach a point of total despair something happens. I just started freely to sculpt the space, not knowing, not worrying any more what it meant. The metaphors and images of house, throne, horse and sword that I was working with all seemed to go into the subconscious, dissolving into pure shapes, geometry and space. One can interpret, one can guess, but no meaning can be definitely established or fixed.

On the other hand, **Saint Francis of Assisi** is not really an opera in a traditional sense. It's closer to oratorio, a series of tableaux inspired by Giotto's frescos in Assisi. It is between six and seven hours long and presents the most incredible challenge. There were four main sources of inspiration for me: the city of Assisi; Bellini's painting of Saint Francis; early Renaissance painting and Russian icons.

1

Tsypin describes **The Rhinegold** as the beginning and the end of the world at the same time, with a pervading revolutionary feel, reminiscent of the Russian early 20th-century avant guard: "And why not? Wasn't Wagner himself a revolutionary at some point, and isn't the **Ring Cycle** a precursor to the bloody, apocalyptic 20th century?" Medieval and alchemical imagery, the legends that inspired Wagner's understanding of creation, dictated the choice of materials for **The Rhinegold**: "The whole physical world of the show is a drama-clash of materials: metal, stone, wood and glass, as if we are Gods and *Nibelungs* in the story, trying to mix these ingredients to make the gold or forge the magic sword. I created three enormous square platforms, constantly moving in space; two – water and sky – were made of glass, and the earth was steel. The mirror-like, shimmering surface of brushed aluminium in the back suggests unattainable Valhalla. Can we really understand what the Gods are building?"

RING CYCLE: THE RHINEGOLD
By Richard Wagner
Netherlands Opera, Het
Muziektheater, Amsterdam, 1997
Directed by Pierre Audi

1 Production photo: Finale,
Rhinegold Rainbow Bridge
2 Model: The basic set
3 Production photo: Act III
4 Production photo: Act I

2

3

4

1

"In **The Valkyries** we find ourselves in a more sensual natural world. Wood is the dominant material. The disk made of bent wood suggests the cut of the tree as well as the moon. The orchestra is cut into the disk and the strange steel shapes are thrust into the tree: perhaps this is the sword left for Siegmund by Wotan? His spear floats above the audience; it will crush the sword when his son Siegmund has to die. In the famous ride of the Valkyries we don't see the horses: we only see the lines of fire left by their vicious feet. The dancing fire seems totally alive, out of control, magic: you rarely see something like this on stage."

RING CYCLE: THE VALKYRIES
By Richard Wagner
Netherlands Opera, Het
Muziektheater, Amsterdam, 1997
Directed by Pierre Audi

1 Production photo: Act I, The sword of Sigmund is crushed
2 Production photo: Act III, The ride of the Valkyries
3 Production photo: Act III, The ride of the Valkyries
4 Model: The basic set

2

3

4

"The design for **The Twilight of the Gods**, the final opera of the **Ring Cycle**, is dominated by a kind of falling Tower of Babel. Curved walls of steel and wood create an energetic downward-upward thrust. Some of the audience members are placed on these walls, sitting in so-called 'adventure seats'. Watching the show from this angle is a mind-altering experience. An endless stone beam is hovering above the house and eventually crushes the glass floor. And it's this floor that is rising as piles and piles of glass shards of ice: the flood. Finally comes the image of burning Valhalla; the flames completely surround the stage; Wotan's spear is on fire as it breaks through the wall. And then the most amazing thing happens. Thousands of fluorescent lights, unnoticed before, light the audience, the balconies and the entire theatre. We feel the theatre itself is on fire, that Valhalla is us. The circle is complete."

RING CYCLE: THE TWILIGHT OF THE GODS
By Richard Wagner
Netherlands Opera, Het
Muziektheater, Amsterdam, 1997
Directed by Pierre Audi

1 Production photo: Back side of the set

"The world of **Siegfried** is even more twisted, complex and schizophrenic. It's as if we have entered the magic forest, crossroads, Siegfried's subconscious. Later the main road seemingly made of one steel blade, starts to move, to bend and wakes up as the dragon. And then, out of nowhere, the magic circle of fire surrounding Brunnhilda appears but this fire is made of glass, which in this **Ring Cycle** seems to become fire, water and sky at different times. Steel can become a forest, wood could be the earth and real fire is a pure emotion."

RING CYCLE: SIEGFRIED
By Richard Wagner
Netherlands Opera, Het
Muziektheater, Amsterdam, 1997
Directed by Pierre Audi

1 Model: The basic set
2 Production photo: Act 1
3 Production photo: Act 2, The Dragon

1

The set for **Saint Francis of Assisi** consisted of four parts. Tsypin constructed the skeletal remains of an enormous cathedral which would house a chorus of 150 people. "It was a cathedral in the process of being built or being destroyed; exploding, crushing through the mountain, flying into the cosmos. The inspiration here is the actual structure of Gothic cathedrals, icons, Russian Constructivism, the freedom of dreaming in space. The floor and the cliff are stylised, made of wood, with jagged lines as in Byzantine painting. The dominance of untreated, bare wood overall is shocking. It makes you think of the cross, of the naked body of Christ. And then a square structure of thousands of fluorescent lights: constantly changing patterns and colour, pulsing, vulgar, impossible, sickening. It's the sky of the inflamed mind inspired by the background in those medieval illuminated manuscripts. The actual scenes are played with the little constructions made of television sets: they become little caves, rooms, churches and coffins."

6

7

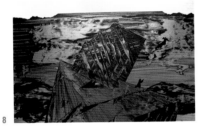

8

ST FRANCIS OF ASSISI
By Olivier Messiaen
Salzburg Festival, Austria and
the Bastille Opera, Paris,
France, 1992
Directed by Peter Sellars

1 Construction photo: Building the
replica cathedral
2 Production photo: The light
structure
3, 4 Construction photos: The
replica cathedral
5 Construction photo: The replica
cathedral with suspended
television screens
6 Research material: Tsypin's own
copy of Tatlin's Tower, the
Memorial to the Third
International, 1922
7 Research material: Example of
the kind of Byzantine icon that
influenced Tsypin's work
8 Painting: Tsypin's own work
which explores the themes in
this production

My first influence came from Assisi itself; driving up the mountains approaching Assisi is the most unforgettable experience. The city seems completely unattainable – you are not sure whether the vision is real. Then, all of a sudden, a breathtaking 360-degree panorama opens up and you've reached the peak of the mountain. You are exhausted, dizzy, the vertigo makes you nauseous, the sky is psychedelic, the landscape is hallucinatory. That's the atmosphere I wanted to capture in this production. When I say 'atmosphere', I don't mean enormous backdrops or styrofoam mountains. I mean the feeling I just described, of being at the edge of this world, the feeling of being allowed a glimpse at another world.

How do you do this on stage? After months of struggling in vain, I stumbled upon an interesting observation in the book called 'The Meaning of Icons'. For centuries the dominant opinion was that the icon painters, because of their ignorance of perspective and their 'primitive' approach to painting, drew this funny architecture as a background for the main figures on the painting. But if you study it more carefully, you realise that you can't draw something like this by mistake. It represents a surreal, 'beyond sense' approach to space that clearly points to the supernatural, other-worldly character of what is going on. Something clicked. Once again, as long as I was able to abandon any remnants of illustration, literary narrative, anything rational in fact, the space started to speak.

When I worked on Prokofiev's opera, **War and Peace**, I decided to put the entire action on the earth and in the cosmos, the sky. In the Russian language the word for 'peace' and for 'the world' is the same. However, the spelling used to be a little different before the reform of the language in 1917. Apparently, when Leo Tolstoy wrote *War and Peace* he really meant 'War and the World'. Whether true or not, there is no question that he was dealing with the world in the novel.

I had been obsessing about the globe shape for a while. It suggested the shape of Russian onion domes and a pregnant woman's body. I started thinking of layering – the idea of the earth as a human body, the layers of clothing or even skin, being stripped away. So the whole of 'Peace', the first Act, takes place on a strangely curved, convex parquet floor. It gives all the interior scenes an eerie, surreal feel. In the ball scene the enormous number of people dancing on the globe feels like the world on the edge of a precipice. And yet it also gives you a very contemporary cinematic perception of a fish-eye lens, so somehow you are getting a close-up and long shot at the same time. The world of 'Peace' is seen through Natasha's eyes and is childish, fragile and magical. There are glass columns, planets almost like Christmas toys and distant stars.

In the second Act, the earth crushes and breaks open, revealing corpses and mutilated bodies. It shows an earth which is bloodied, real, with the material showing remnants of endless wars and suffering. The sky, by contrast, was magic, esoteric, dreamlike, ephemeral and constantly changing. It is the famous 'tall' sky, the way that dying Andrei Bolkonski sees it when he is fatally wounded in the field of battle. People's actions, destinies and lives seem small and

1

War and Peace achieved some notoriety at the Kirov opening because of the extreme demands the production made of the theatre and because of the unusual nature of Tsypin's vision. This radical design takes care to reflect the images and subject of **War and Peace**. An architect will often work through research, metaphors and great detail in order to create a building. Tsypin's work reveals an architect's attempt to give comprehensive consideration to all of the issues in order that the solution can be as effective as possible. The epic can still be presented in a way that captures an audience's imagination by offering them something unexpected and arresting.

5

6

WAR AND PEACE
By Sergei Prokofiev
Co-production by the Kirov Opera
of St Petersburg, Russia, and the
Metropolitan Opera, New York,
USA, 2000
Directed by Andrei Konchalovsky

1 Model: Act I. The Ball
2, 3 Models: Act II. Fire of
Moscow
4 Model: Act II
5 Model: Act II. Vision of Moscow
6 Model: Act I

inconsequential next to this sky. That overall set-up immediately gave an epic dimension to the whole performance. As for the vision of sacred Moscow behind the sky, nobody could believe the audacity of putting most of the sets – that is, the expense – behind the plastic drop, so all the audience could see was a faint mirage of the sacred city Moscow or what's beyond the sky. It's Moscow, which every Russian was willing to burn, so that Napoleon could not conquer it. It is a Moscow that is no longer there, a spiritual dimension of the people.

The visual influences for a design can come from many sources. When I designed for the two live performances of Stravinsky's short opera, **Oedipus Rex**, the fact that it was also conceived as a film to be shot on location in Japan in many ways determined the shape of the production. With its enormous chorus, masks, puppets and narrator, it is a monumental presentation of Sophocles' play as well as of the myth. The opera is an oratorio; a series of tableaux are interrupted by the narration of the story. People look like sculptures; sculptures like people; masks make everyone look like ghosts: it's the world of the dead. When Oedipus pokes his eyes out, the entire surrounding mountain disappears as a scrim and an enormous red silk is released from the flies. As a member of the audience, you feel your eyes are bloodied, you go blind. In the next tableaux, Oedipus and the chorus go into the underworld of the black water and ritual fire, with the final tremendous music.

Realising a project of this scale is always a nightmare. The three bids that I got from Japanese construction shops were for nine million dollars. Finally I was able to build for much less in America. When the black mirror that I wanted at the bottom of the pool was installed and the stage was getting filled with water, one of the most magical moments occurred. In the moment of collective euphoria, everyone rushed into the water, the light was bouncing all over the rocks: it was spectacular. Two hours later, I returned to the theatre. All of the mirror that had been glued to the bottom of the pool was strangely warped and came up above the surface of the water like a school of whales. It was ominous and ugly. The whole multi-million dollar production was in danger. Materials have their own logic sometimes and there is nothing you can do. There is no question that, as a designer, you often carry the entire weight of the production on your shoulders.

For me design is the search for that hidden formal mechanism, the sculptural 'melody' of the space. I constantly have to do a parallel formal exploration in my sculptural work. The two – design and sculpture – feed on each other. Sculpture in a way is building a model without the constraints of real theatrical space; it's trying to capture 'other space' that in theatre is implied but often remains in your imagination. It's a search in terms of spatial solutions but also in terms of materials and the use of light and real objects. For me the model itself is a very autonomous work of art. It has to have an integrity of its own. When building a sculpture or a model, I use glass, steel, wood and stones. My sculptures seem to be inhabited by invisible people or strange mythical creatures. But, they are not there: they'll show up later...on stage.

Tsypin describes the Japanese use of wood as an influence for the set for **Oedipus Rex**: "The set is a gigantic eye, made of bent wood. In the middle of the space there is a floating disc that is moving in different directions. Sometimes we see the dancer as the spirit of Oedipus on it, sometimes his mother, Jocasta. On that disc she eventually commits suicide." The stage represents the black lake with a wooden construction floating above. It's surrounded by rocks made of crinkled mosquito netting, which has a very three-dimensional and yet eerie, ephemeral feeling: "It reflects in the water, creating a terrifying bottomless well. The main structure at times looks like a mythic bird or a strange spider-like animal. The wings of that bird appear to move under the feet of the chorus. The place seemed mysterious, sick and cursed."

3

OEDIPUS REX
Text by Jean Cocteau
Composed by Igor Stravinsky
Saito Kine Festival, Matsamoto,
Japan, 1992
Directed by Julie Taymor

1 Production still: The left side of
the stage, showing the reflections
in the water
2 Production still: Steps to
the stage
3 Model: The gigantic eye

Günther Schneider-Siemssen

2001 **The Four Seasons**, Vivaldi, Landestheatre, Salzburg, Austria

2000/1 **The Ring Cycle**, Dir: Schneider-Siemssen, Wagner Festival, Wels, Austria

1999 **Tristan**, Wagner, Wagner Festival, Wels, Austria, & Festival of Light, Salzburg, Austria

1998 **Dracula**, World Premiere, Munich Art Concerts, Open Air at Hanover, Vienna & Munich; Awarded the Cross of Honour for achievements in the Arts and Sciences of Austria

1996 **Fidelio**, Beethoven, Aachen Theatre, Aachen, Germany

1995 **Don Giovanni**, Mozart, Aachen Theatre, Aachen, Germany; Rigoletto, Verdi, Arena of Verona, Verona, Italy

1993/4 **Ariadne auf Naxos**, Strauss, Dir: August Everding, Theatre Colón, Buenos Aires, Argentina; **Jenufa**, Janácek, Dir: August Everding, Theatre Colón, Buenos Aires, Argentina

1992 **Tristan**, Wagner, Wagner Festival, Wels, Austria; Tosca, Puccini, Easter Festival, Salzburg, Austria

1991 **Palestrina**, Pierluigi, City Theatre, Hannover, Germany; Rusalker, Houston, USA; Parsifal, Metropolitan Opera, New York, USA

1990 **The Passion of John Wade**, Houston, Miami, San Diego, USA

1987 Awarded the Medal of Honour by the City of Vienna, Austria; Honorary Doctorate of the Inter American University for Humanistic Science, Calvatone, Cremona, Italy

Ralph Koltai

2000 Special Award for Distinguished Service to the Theatre, United Institute for Theatre Technology, USA

1997 **Simon Boccanegra**, Verdi, Dir: David Pountney, Welsh National Opera, UK

1993 **Hair**, Rado and Radni, Dir: Michael Bogdanov, The Old Vic, London, UK

1991 **The Makropoulos Affair**, Janácek, Dir: Keith Warner, Norwegian Opera, Norway

1990 **The Planets**, Dir: David Bintley, The Royal Ballet, Royal Opera House, London, UK

1984 **Cyrano de Bergerac**, Royal Shakespeare Company, Los Angeles/New York, USA (Designer of the Year Award, Society of West End Theatre, London, UK)

1983 CBE Award

1978 **The Seven Deadly Sins**, Weill, Chor: Richard Alston, English National Opera, London, UK; **Brand**, Ibsen, Dir: Christopher Morahan, Royal National Theatre, London, UK (Designer of the Year Award, Society of West End Theatre, London, UK)

1977 **Cruel Garden**, Bruce and Kemp, Ballet Rambert, Round House, London, UK

1967 **Little Murders**, Feiffer, Dir: Christopher Morahan, Royal Shakespeare Company, Stratford, UK (London Drama Critics Award); **As You Like It**, Shakespeare, Dir: Clifford Williams, Royal National Theatre, London, UK (London Drama Critics Award)

1966 **Diversities**, Badings, Dir: Jonathan Taylor, Ballet Rambert, London, UK

1965 **The Tribute**, Sessions, Dir: Norman Morrice, The Royal Ballet Touring Company

1950 **Angélique**, Ibert, Dir: Geoffrey Dunn, Fortune Theatre, London, UK

Ming Cho Lee

2000 **Guys and Dolls**, Loesser, Dir: Richard Hamburger, Dallas Theatre Centre, USA

1998 **Angels in America**, Parts 1 and 2, Kushner, Dir: Richard Hamburger, Dallas Theatre Centre, USA

1997 **Portrait of the Families**, Dir: Lin Hwai-Min, Cloud Gate Dance Theatre, Taipei, Taiwan

1995 **Mourning Becomes Electra**, O'Neill, Dir: Michael Kahn, Shakespeare Theatre, Washington DC, USA; OBIE for Sustained Achievement

1993 **Nine Songs**, Dir: Lin Hwai-Min, Cloud Gate Dance Theatre, Taipei, Taiwan

1989 Distinguished Artist Fellowship (National Endowment for the Arts Theatre Programme)

1987 **Romeo and Juliet**, Dir: Kent Stowell, Pacific Northwest Ballet, USA; Guggenheim Fellowship, New York, USA; Peter Zeisler Award for Distinguished Achievement in the American Theatre

1984 Mayor's Award for Arts and Culture, New York, USA

1983 **K2**, Meyers, Broadway, New York, USA (Tony Award, Outer Critics Circle Award, Drama Desk Award and Maharam Award)

1980 National Opera Institute Special Award for Service to American Opera

1976 **Lohengrin**, Wagner, Dir: August Everding, Metropolitan Opera, New York, USA

1974 **Boris Godunov**, Mussorgsky, Dir: August Everding, Metropolitan Opera, New York, USA

1967 **Hair**, Dir: Gerald Freedman, Public Theatre, New York, USA

1962 New York Shakespeare Theatre, Principal Designer

Guy-Claude François

2000   **Tambours sur la Digue**, Dir: Ariane Mnouchkine, Théâtre du Soleil, La Cartoucherie, Paris, France

1994   **La Ville Parjure**, Dir: Ariane Mnouchkine, Théâtre du Soleil, La Cartoucherie, Paris, France

1992   **Life is a Dream**, Calderón de la Barca, Dir: O. Krejca, Théâtre de Vasteras, Stockholm, Sweden; **The Miser**, Molière, dir: O. Krejca, Théâtre de Vasteras, Stockholm, Sweden

1990   **Les Atrides**, Dir: Ariane Mnouchkine, Théâtre du Soleil, La Cartoucherie, Paris, France; **Terre Étrangère**, Schnitzler, Dir: O. Krejca, National Theatre of Finland, Helsinki, Finland

1989   **The Misanthrope**, Molière, Dir: A. Delecampe, Atelier Théâtral, Brussels, Belgium

1987   **L'Indiade**, Dir: Ariane Mnouchkine, Théâtre du Soleil, La Cartoucherie, Paris, France

1981   **Les Shakespeares**, Dir: Ariane Mnouchkine, Théâtre du Soleil, La Cartoucherie, Paris, France

1979   **Mephisto**, Dir: Ariane Mnouchkine, Théâtre du Soleil, La Cartoucherie, Paris, France

1975   **L'Age d'Or**, Dir: Ariane Mnouchkine, Théâtre du Soleil, La Cartoucherie, Paris, France

Jaroslav Malina

2000   **Othello**, Shakespeare, Dir: Ivan Balada, Municipal Theatre, Zlin, Czech Republic

1999   **The Government Inspector**, Gogol, Dir: Ivan Balada, Municipal Theatre, Zlin, Czech Republic

1998   **Come Nasce il Sogetto Cinematographico**, Zavattini, Dir: Ivan Balada, Municipal Theatre, Zlin, Czech Republic

1996   **La Folle de Chaillot**, Giraudoux, Dir: Ivan Balada, Municipal Theatre, Zlin, Czech Republic;

1994   **The Cunning Little Vixen**, Janácek, Dir: David Sulkin, SD Ostrava, Czech Republic

1990   **The Insect Play**, Capek, Dir: Miroslav Krobot, National Theatre, Prague, Czech Republic

1988   **Merlin**, Dorst, Dir: Miroslav Krobot, RDZN (Annual Prize for Best Production Nomination, Government of the Czech Republic)

1984   **A Midsummer Night's Dream**, Shakespeare, Dir: Karel Kriz, MDP-ABC (Gold Medal, 7th International Triennial of Stage Design and Theatrical Costuming, Novi Sad, Yugoslavia)

1981   Annual Prize, Union of Czech Dramatic Artists, National Festival of Works, Czech Republic

1979   **Troilus and Cressida**, Shakespeare, Dir: Ivan Rajmont, Cinoherni Studio, Usti nad Labem, Czech Republic

William Dudley

2000   **The Silver Tassie**, Turnage, Dir: Bill Bryden, English National Opera, London, UK

1998   **Amadeus**, Schaffer, Dir: Peter Hall, The Old Vic, London, UK/Los Angeles and New York, USA (Laurence Olivier Award)

1997   **The Homecoming**, Pinter, Dir: Roger Michell, Royal National Theatre, London, UK

1994   **The Big Picnic**, Bryden, Dir: Bill Bryden, Promenade Productions, Harland & Wolff Shipyard, Glasgow, UK

1990   **The Cunning Little Vixen**, Janácek, Dir: Bill Bryden, Royal Opera House, London, UK; **The Ship**, Bryden, Dir: Bill Bryden, Promenade Productions, Harland & Wolff Shipyard, Glasgow, UK (Theatre Crafts International Award)

1987   **The Shaughraun**, Bouccicault, Dir: Howard Davies, Royal National Theatre, London, UK (Plays and Players Award)

1985   **The Futurists**, Hughes, Dir: Richard Eyre, Royal National Theatre, London, UK (Laurence Olivier Award and Time Out Award); **The Merry Wives of Windsor**, Shakespeare, Dir: Bill Alexander, Royal Shakespeare Company, Stratford/London, UK (Drama Award and Laurence Olivier Award)

1984   **The Critic**, Sheridan, Dir: Sheila Hancock, Royal National Theatre, London, UK (Drama Award and Laurence Olivier Award)

1980   **Hamlet**, Shakespeare, Dir: Richard Eyre, Royal Court, London, UK (Drama Award)

1977   **The Mysteries**, Harrison, Dir: Bill Bryden, Royal National Theatre, London/Edinburgh, UK (Plays and Players Award, Drama Award and Olivier Award)

Maria Björnson

2000   **The Cherry Orchard**, Chekhov, Dir: Trevor Nunn, Royal National Theatre, London, UK
1998   **Plenty**, Hare, Dir: Jonathan Kent, Almeida Theatre, London, UK; **Britannicus**, Racine, Dir: Jonathan Kent, Almeida Theatre, London, UK
1997   **Macbeth**, Verdi, Dir: Graham Vick, La Scala, Milan, Italy
1991   **The Blue Angel**, Jems, Dir: Trevor Nunn, Royal Shakespeare Company, The Other Place, Stratford, UK
1990   **The Rise and Fall of the City of Mahogany**, Weil, Dir: Graham Vick, Verdi Theatre, Maggio Musicale, Florence, Italy (Expert's Expert and The Designers' Designer Award for contribution to Theatre Design, The Observer, London, UK)
1987   **Follies**, Sondheim, Dir: Mike Ockrent, The Shaftesbury Theatre, London, UK (Best Design, Drama Magazine 1988); **The Phantom of the Opera**, Lloyd Webber, Dir: Harold Prince, Her Majesty's Theatre, London, UK (Best Design, Drama Magazine 1987, Best Set/Costumes, Tony Awards 1987–1988 and Best Set/Costumes, Drama Critics Award, Los Angeles)
1983   **The Valkyries**, Wagner, Dir: David Pountney, English National Opera, London, UK (Prague Biennial Prize and Silver Medal, Janácek Competition, Prague Quadrennial)
1981   **The Makropoulos Affair**, Janácek, Dir: David Pountney, Scottish Opera and Welsh National Opera, UK
1979   **Katya Kabanova**, Janácek, Dir: David Pountney, Scottish Opera and Welsh National Opera, UK

JC Serroni

2000   **The Rascal's Opera**, de Hollanda, Dir: Gabriel Villela, TBC Musical Repertoire Company, Brazilian Comedy Theatre, São Paulo, Brazil; **King Lear**, Shakespeare, Dir: Ron Daniels, SESC Vila Mariana Theatre, São Paulo, Brazil
1995   **Gilgamesh**, Filho, Dir: Antunes Filho, Macunaima Group, Anchieta Theatre, São Paulo, Brazil; **Dracula and Other Vampires**, Filho, Dir: Antunes Filho, Macunaima Group, Anchieta Theatre, São Paulo, Brazil (Golden Triga for Brazilian Exhibition, Prague Quadrennial and ITI Award)
1991   **Zero**, Brandao, Dir: Hans Kresnik, São Paulo City Ballet, Municipal Theatre, São Paulo, Brazil; **New Old Story**, Filho, Dir: Antunes Filho, Macunaima Group, Anchieta Theatre, São Paulo, Brazil
1990   **The Coffee Trade Foxes**, Bivar and Paulini, Dir: Eduardo Tolentino, Tapa Group, Alainca Francesa Theatre, São Paulo, Brazil
1989   **Nelson 2 Rodrigues**, Filho, Dir: Antunes Filho, Macunaima Group, Spanish Repertory Theatre, New York, USA; **North Side Paradise**, Filho, Dir: Antunes Filho, Macunaima Group, Anchieta Theatre, São Paulo, Brazil
1985   **Saint Joan**, Shaw, Dir: Jose Possi Neto, Auditorio Elis Regina Theatre, São Paulo, Brazil
1984   **Hamlet**, Shakespeare, Dir: Marcio Aurelio, Sergio Cardoso Theatre, São Paulo, Brazil
1982   **Accidental Death of an Anarchist**, Fo, Dir: Antonio Abujamra, Stable Repertoire Company, Brazilian Comedy Theatre, São Paulo, Brazil

Yukio Horio

2000   **The Memory of Water**, Noda, Dir: Hideki Noda, Cocoon Theatre, Tokyo, Japan; **The Miracle Worker**, Dir: Yumi Suzuki, Hori Pro Company, Cocoon Theatre, Tokyo, Japan (Kinikuniya Theatre Arts Award, Japan)
1999   **Pandora's Bell**, Noda, Dir: Hideki Noda, Setagaya Public Theatre, Tokyo, Japan; **King Lear**, Shakespeare, Dir: Yukio Ninagawa, Royal Shakespeare Company, Barbican Theatre, London/Royal Shakespeare Theatre, Stratford, UK (6th Yomiuri Theatre Arts Award for Best Cast, Japan)
1998   **Buddha**, Osamu, Dir: Tamiya Kuriyama, New National Theatre, Tokyo, Japan; **Romeo and Juliet**, Shakespeare, Dir: Yukio Ninagawa, Saitama Arts Theatre, Saitama, Japan
1996   **Taboo**, Noda, Dir: Hideki Noda, Cocoon Theatre, Toyko, Japan (3rd Yomiuri Theatre Arts Award for Best Cast, Japan)
1995   **Ghetto**, Dir: Tamiya Kuriyama, Performing Arts Project Hyogo, Shin-Kobe Oriental Theatre, Kobe, Japan; **Yuzuru Opera**, Dan, Dir: Masayoshi Kuriyama, Gakugeki-Kyokai Japan, Municipal Theatre, São Paulo, Brazil
1993   **Grease Paint**, Inoue, Dir: Kouichi Kimura, Lyric Chijinkai Company, The Lyric Theatre, London, UK; **The Rhinegold**, Wagner, Dir: Keiichi Nishizawa, Nikikai Opera Theatre Company, Tokyo Bunka Kaikan Theatre, Japan
1991   **Ogurihangan Terute-hime**, Dir: Takuo Endo, Yokohama Boat Theatre Company, The Cathedral of St John, New York, USA; Kisaku Ito Award for Outstanding Achievement in Theatre Arts, Japan
1983   **Lucia di Lammermoor**, Donizetti, Dir: Yasuhiko Aguni, Fujiwara Opera Company, Tokyo Bunka Kaikan Theatre, Japan

Richard Hudson

2000 **Cosi Fan Tutte**, Mozart, Dir: Graham Vick, Glyndebourne Festival Opera, Glyndebourne, UK; **The Marriage of Figaro**, Mozart, Dir: Graham Vick, Glyndebourne Festival Opera, Glyndebourne, UK; **Don Giovanni**, Mozart, Dir: Graham Vick, Glyndebourne Festival Opera, Glyndebourne, UK

1999 **The Queen of Spades**, Tchaikovsky, Glyndebourne Festival Opera, UK

1997 **Manon Lescaut**, Puccini, Dir: Graham Vick, Glyndebourne Festival Opera, UK; **Die Meistersinger von Nurnberg**, Wagner, Dir: Graham Vick, Royal Opera House, London, UK

1996 **The Cherry Orchard**, Chekhov, Dir: Adrian Noble, Royal Shakespeare Company, The Albery Theatre, London, UK; **Ermione**, Rossini, Dir: Graham Vick, Glyndebourne Festival Opera, UK

1995 **The Rake's Progress**, Stravinsky, Dir: Graham Vick, Chicago Lyric Opera, USA

1993 **The Tales of Hoffman**, Offenbach, Dir: Andrei Serban, Vienna State Opera, Austria

1991 **La Bête**, Hirson, Dir: Richard Jones, The Lyric Theatre, New York, USA

1990 **Too Clever by Half**, Ostrovsky, Dir: Richard Jones, The Old Vic, London, UK (Laurence Olivier Award);

1989 **The Master Builder**, Ibsen, Dir: Adrian Noble, Royal Shakespeare Company, The Albery Theatre, London, UK

1987 **A Night at the Chinese Opera**, Weir, Dir: Richard Jones, Kent Opera, UK

Adrianne Lobel

2000 **Cellini**, Shanley, Dir: John Patrick Shanley, The Second Stage Theatre, New York, USA

1997 **The Diary of Anne Frank**, Kesselman, Dir: James Lapine, Music Box Theatre, New York, USA; **On the Town**, Bernstein, Dir: George C Wolfe, The Delacorte Theatre, New York, USA; **Lady in the Dark**, Weil, Dir: Francesca Zambello, Royal National Theatre, London, UK; **Platée**, Rameau, Dir: Mark Morris, Royal Opera House, London, UK

1996 **The Rake's Progress**, Stravinsky, Dir: Peter Sellars, Chatelet Opera, Paris, France

1995 **Orfeo ed Euridice**, Gluck, Chor: Mark Morris, USA Tour 1996

1989 **L'Allegro, il Penseroso ed il Moderato**, Handel, Chor: Mark Morris, Royal Exchange Theatre, Brussels, Belgium

1994 **Passion**, Sonheim/Lapine, Dir: James Lapine, Broadway, New York, USA; **Street Scene**, Weil, Dir: Francesca Zambello, Grand Opera, Houston, USA

1990 **Lohengrin**, Wagner, Dir: Anja Silja, Royal Exchange Theatre, Brussels, Belgium

1988 **The Marriage of Figaro**, Mozart, Dir: Peter Sellars, Pepsico Summerfare, Purchase, New York, USA

1987 **Nixon in China**, Adams and Goodman, Dir: Peter Sellars, Grand Opera, Houston, USA

1986 **Cosi Fan Tutte**, Mozart, Dir: Peter Sellars, Pepsico Summerfare, Purchase, New York, USA

1984 **The Vampires**, Kondoleon, Dir: Kondoleon, Astor Place Theatre, New York, USA

1980 **La Traviata**, Verdi, Dir: Andrei Serban, The Julliard School, New York, USA

George Tsypin

2000 **L'Amour de Loin**, Sarajaho, Salzburg Festival, Austria

1999 **The Biblical Pieces**, Stravinsky, Dir: Peter Sellars, Netherlands Opera, Amsterdam, Holland

1998 **La Pericole**, Offenbach, Dir: Jurgen Flimm, Zurich Opera, Switzerland; **Le Grand Macabre**, Ligeti and de Ghelerode, Salzburg Festival, Austria

1997 **Theodora**, Handel, Dir: Peter Sellars, Glyndebourne Festival Opera, UK

1996 **The Gambler**, Prokofiev, Dir: Timur Chkheidze, La Scala, Milan, Italy

1995 **Mathis der Maler**, Hindemith, Dir: Peter Sellars, Royal Opera House, London, UK: **The Flying Dutchman**, Wagner, Dir: Julie Taymor, Los Angeles Opera, USA

1993 **Pelleas and Melisande**, Debussy, Dir: Peter Sellars, Netherlands Opera, Amsterdam, Holland; **The Magic Flute**, Mozart, Dir: Julie Taymor, Municipal Theatre, Florence, Italy

1991/2 **The Death of Klinghoffer**, Adams and Goodman, Dir: Peter Sellars, Netherlands Opera, Brussels, Belgium/Vienna, Austria/Lyons, France/San Francisco and New York, USA

1990 OBIE for Sustained Excellence

1989 **Don Giovanni**, Mozart, Dir: Peter Sellars, Pepsico Summerfare, Purchase, New York, USA

1988 **Tannhauser**, Wagner, Dir: Peter Sellars, Chicago Lyric Opera, USA; **The Screens**, Genet, Dir: Joanne Akalaitis, The Guthrie Theatre, Minneapolis, USA

1987 **The Electrification of the Soviet Union**, Osborne and Raine, Glyndebourne Festival Opera, UK; **Leon and Lena**, Buchner, Dir: Joanne Akalaitis, The Guthrie Theatre, Minneapolis, USA

1985 **Idiot's Delight**, Sherwood, Dir: Peter Sellars, American National Theatre, Kennedy Centre, Washington, USA

Abstract Expressionism: An American 1950s' art practice, often produced on large canvases, that usually did not seek to represent the world and the objects in it. It emerged as an all-American art form at the height of the Cold War and was strongly advocated by key critics. Along with movies and jazz, it was one of the great American achievements of the 20th century. It is commented upon by both Ming Cho Lee (p40) and William Dudley (p78). See also Figurative Art.

Act: One of the primary divisions of a play written since the Renaissance in the Western tradition. Roman numerals are often used: Act I, II, III, IV and V for Act 1, 2, 3, 4 and 5.

Action Design or Action Scenography: An approach to design most closely identified with Jaroslav Malina (pp62–75), that aims to eliminate superfluous decoration on the stage and instead to create an abstract space that is linked to the dramatic action in poetic and metaphoric ways. Instead of illustrative design, action scenography produces meaning from the combination of actor, set, costume and other performance elements. The scenographer becomes a more active partner in creating a production. Action design, with its use of 'real' objects, only makes sense during the course of a performance, when it comes to life.

Audience: An English term for those who attend a play, although its origin is the verb 'to listen'. In France those who attend performances are 'spectators', which is perhaps more appealing from a stage design point of view.

Auditorium: Usually the part of a theatre that the audience occupy.

Black: Richard Hudson refers to 'a piece of black' being used to cover up some of the set (p138). This may be a flat, it may be flown, or it may be draped over part of the set. A black can be used to make parts of the set appear to vanish.

Costume Shop: A workshop either attached to a theatre or in another location, where costumes are made.

Cyclorama: A stretched cloth, usually from floor to ceiling and usually white, that creates a concave wall at the back of the scenic space on a stage. Lighter, neutral colours like white and pale grey can be transformed by any colour directed onto them. A cyclorama provides a versatile backdrop that can be transformed by lighting.

Designer: For the purposes of this book, see Stage Designer. Otherwise it could refer to a lighting designer, costume designer, make-up designer, mask designer etc. See also Scenographer.

Director: The person who leads the actors and combines their practice with the work of the stage, lighting, sound and other designers. At times the source of ideas for a play, at other times more of a team player, especially in relation to a scenographer.

Drafting: The process of drawing up technical plans and elevations to show what will be required in order that a set can be constructed.

Dramaturg: Someone attached to a theatre or to a theatre company who advises on the nature and shape of new work. In the UK, this function tends to be carried out in a rather different way by script editors or literary managers.

Elevation: A scale drawing of a set made in projection on a vertical plane – the anatomised view of a set from the side.

Expressionism: A term used to describe a variety of strongly expressive 20th-century art forms. It emerged before the First World War in 1914 from the work of artists like Edvard Munch (see p92) who used pronounced line, form and colour to express emotional states in as direct a manner as possible. Later, in Germany especially, expressionism became a popular mode for visual artists, poets and film-makers. A key expressionist film was Robert Wiene's *The Cabinet of Dr Caligari*, 1917, a black and white film notable for the angularity of its designs; another was Fritz Lang's *Metropolis*, 1929, (see p36). The style was carried into the Hollywood movie industry by expatriate German film-makers and was a hallmark of film noir from the 1940s onwards.

Figurative Art: Art and design that seeks to represent the world and the objects in it, including the human figure. It was going out of fashion in the 1950s and 1960s when Ming Cho Lee and William Dudley were being trained; American abstract expressionism was favoured instead. During the 1960s William Dudley, at St Martin's School of Art, found that other students would rub their fingers in his damp, oil-painted figurative canvases, leaving abusive texts and that staff did not favour figurative approaches. This indicated that the fine art world and its colleges were a willing target for American cultural imperialism rather than managing a diverse practise. This led to Bill and a group of fellow student exiles setting up their own cheap workshop to learn the practise of figurative painting. See also Abstract Expressionism.

Flats: A rectangular wooden frame covered with material, often used as a vertical border extending from the wing onto the stage. In post-Renaissance theatres, there might be four or so pairs of flats symmetrically placed on either side of the stage. As they go upstage away from the audience, so they actually or appear to diminish in size, articulating the receding perspective. Flats may be flown or free-standing.

Fly, Flying, Flown: Many theatres can lift out and drop in scenery and objects that are supported by rope. This is called flying. There is a counterweight system that makes it easier to manage great weights. It is still a manual system in many theatres. A good example of a famous, large-scale scene change that is flown is the arrival of the US president's plane, Air Force One, in Act 1 of John Adams' opera, **Nixon in China**. See Adrianne Lobel's chapter (pp150–151).

Gauze: A translucent fabric which can be lit from in front, so that it appears as a solid and opaque plane, or from behind, so that it becomes almost transparent. Known in the US as scrim.

Holography: The projection of a virtual, three-dimensional image. Currently it tends to occur on the smaller scale. See Günther Schneider-Siemssen's chapter (pp14–25).

Kabuki: A traditional form of Japanese popular theatre that was frowned upon by the authorities and reached its peak in 18th-century Edo (Tokyo). Like Noh Theatre, it is presented according to specific conventions. See also Noh Theatre.

Italian-style Theatre: A theatre with a proscenium arch and a scenic stage. See also Proscenium Arch and Scenic Stage.

Librettist: Responsible for the words and perhaps the structure of an opera.

Masque: A European courtly entertainment which reached a peak of achievement in relation to the post-Renaissance theatre of perspective, wings and idealised imaginary scenic spaces. A masque is a kind of collage drama consisting of sung and danced sequences which offer an allegory (or metaphor) for an earthly situation. They were usually created for and to glorify the monarch, who would sit in the best position to see the show. One of the issues associated with the perspectival set is that it was best viewed from one central position, which was usually offered to the monarch or to the most powerful person in the room. This has remained a challenge for theatre and stage designers as sets have to offer a tolerably good view to everyone in an auditorium. This also explains some of the subsequent tensions relating to the perspectival set, as it was associated with an idealised and rather anti-democratic cultural practice. See also Perspective, Renaissance and Scenic Stage.

Model: A scale model of a stage design and of the stage area is still the main instrument for communicating designs to production

teams, casts, potential backers, workshops and others. Many theatres specify the kind of models they require in the contracts that they offer stage designers. Models are often of a high standard but may well end up inadvertently trashed in the course of constructing a set.

OISTAT: The International Organisation of Scenographers, Theatre Architects and Technicians, an umbrella body that oversees the Prague Quadriennale and which encourages the development of scenography around the world.

Noh Theatre: An ancient form of Japanese theatre that found its modern form over 700 years ago. It is interesting that Noh, like Kabuki, is a form of theatre known for all of the elements of performance rather than as a text. Noh plays intend to catch the mood of fleeting moments; they have no interest in realism and use theatrical resources with restraint. There are five types of Noh Theatre. As Yukio Horio reveals, the rather unbending weight of tradition can be rather unappealing for a contemporary Japanese artist, though he cannot escape the influence of Noh and Kabuki. Yet for a radical contemporary theatre company like New York's Wooster Group, Noh practice offers appealing source material. See Yukio Horio's chapter (pp114–125).

Painted Backdrops: In the early 20th century these were the height of innovation. When Fokine and Diaghilev brought Les Ballets Russes to Western Europe in 1909, the designs of the painters Roualt, de Chirico, Braque, Matisse and Picasso were a major part of the groundbreaking attraction. In 1917 Picasso's designs for the ballet **Parade** were so extraordinary that the poet Appollinaire coined the term 'surrealism' after seeing it. This tradition stretches to the present through artists like the Australian artist Sydney Nolan and the British artist David Hockney, amongst many others. The painted backdrop also represents the birth of the stage designer. After the occasional efforts of artists to design for the stage, the next step was for dedicated stage designers to appear. Although two of the stage designers in this book, Jaroslav Malina and George Tsypin, still exhibit their work in galleries as artists, they work as virtually full-time designers. During the last three quarters of the 20th century, the stage designer became an artist in her and his own right. This is one of the reasons that the term scenographer was coined and adopted by many, so that a contemporary name could be given to a new art form that was earning respect from the performing arts and from the visual arts.

Perspective: The illusion of three dimensions created on a two-dimensional plane; this became one of the leading visual conventions of the Renaissance. The 'dream space' (see William Dudley's chapter p87) of theatre is the illusionistic space or poetic space at the back of the stage, usually above the stage floor. This Renaissance invention has proved extremely durable and works well with the latest media. See also Renaissance and Trompe l'oeil.

Picture Box Set: A set that 'realistically' recreates or seeks to illustrate a setting on stage, often an interior. It tends to lack the imaginative potential of the dream space or of action design.

Plan or Ground Plan: Scale drawing of a set viewed from overhead.

Poetic Realism: The prevalent convention in America during the 1940s – essentially an illustrative approach to design using painted backdrops.

Postmodernism: A rather unstable term that seems now to describe any approach to culture that combines a variety of elements which might not usually be thought to go together. Postmodernism tends at first to be experienced as a welcome release from logical restraint into more associative thinking. It has been derided for being ironic, for not being political and for privileging the intelligence of people who are extremely culturally competent. On the other hand, for many stage designers, it is how they have always thought and worked. Anyone designing settings and costumes for Shakespeare's **Julius Caesar** has to work out how best to present a play that was originally performed by a male cast, which makes few concessions to ancient Rome and which was originally performed 400 years ago in modern dress on an open stage. It is also difficult to read the play afresh as it is filtered through historical interpretation. For a stage designer, this is the kind of fruitful dilemma they face in one way or another with almost any project. For the stage designers in this book, postmodernism is not a passing style, it is an essential hybrid practice which helps them to communicate the essence of a play to a director, a cast and an audience.

Prague Quadriennale: The international gathering of stage designers held by OISTAT every four years in Prague. It's function is celebratory and competitive rather than a trade show. Groups of designers, organised on a national basis, put together shows that display the best of their country's work over the past four years. It will be held every four years from June 2003.

Production: A term that can be used to describe every kind of show, from opera to theatre, and from musicals to ballet and dance, as well as site-specific work.

Production Photo: A specially-commissioned, often black and white, photograph that records a production for publicity and archival purposes; almost invariably this is of leading performers and rarely of the set.

Promenade Performance: A style of performance found around the world throughout history that has become popular again in theatre and other spaces from the 1960s onwards for performances that move around and amongst an audience, many of whom are free to move about.

Proscenium Arch: This emerged during the Renaissance as the framing device that defined where the viewer should sit to see a perspectival setting properly. It is the rectilinear stage frame within which the curtains hang and before which there is often a forestage. At times it is thought by some to be a constraining feature, keeping the audience separate from the performers but it is also recognised as one of the best ways of articulating the audience and performer relationship. On the ground, there is the performer. In the air, at the back of the stage, framed by the proscenium arch, is the space that can become anywhere. See William Dudley's chapter (pp76–89).

Rehearsal: The period when the actors or singers work with the director on the production; during the rehearsal period the set is usually being built. Set and cast may not meet up until late in the process, although the cast are usually introduced to the ideas, model and sketches for the set at an early rehearsal.

Renaissance: A key point for Western civilisation when a particular kind of subjectivity first appeared. Renaissance highlights for the purposes of this book revolve to a great extent around Shakespeare's plays. His plays created, amongst much else, many characters with rounded personalities as we now understand them in novels and in life. Another important development was of the perspectival set and scenic stage in Italy. Shakespeare's career bridged work on the outdoor, open stage and work shown on the indoor, perspectival stage. See also Scenic Stage and Perspective.

Rendering: Often used to describe a drawing of an idea or of a set outline; renderings can be of the highest quality.

Rep: The repertory system involved a performing and technical ensemble based in one theatre who would turn around productions on a regular, perhaps weekly, basis. This practise had come to an end in many countries by the end of the 20th century. Rep was popular amongst the theatre profession because it offered great variety and presented enormous technical challenges that had to be addressed successfully at great speed. A rep apprenticeship was regarded as a near ideal introduction to the theatre. Opera and ballet are often still presented in rep, theatre less so now.

Revolve: A motorised, circular section of the stage that can turn around independently of the rest of the stage, like a flat wheel or millstone.

Scene: Either a sub-division of an Act (see above) or a stage setting.

Scene Shop: A workshop either attached to a theatre or in another location, where scenery is constructed.

Scenic Stage: The area of the stage upstage (that is, further away from the audience) from the proscenium arch. In this part of the stage there would traditionally be wings on either side, and flats and other devices for representing a perspectival scene. At first, there was a forestage in front of the auditorium; later the forestage was left out – though it keeps returning. See also Thrust Stage.

Scenographer: A contemporary term for a stage designer, most popular in Europe. It was created following Josef Svoboda's striking stage design initiatives during the 1950s and is associated in particular with the Czech Republic and its influential history of innovative theatre during the second half of the 20th century.

Scrim: see Gauze.

Set or Setting: The stage environment created by the stage designer, although the setting can mean the location, period and look chosen for a production.

Stage Designer: Someone who creates sets and often costumes for a performance. The person responsible for how the production will look and develop, often working in partnership with the director. The role may also be as member of a creative ensemble who is responsible for ensuring that the set is delivered.

Storyboard: A sequence of drawings representing the sequence of settings for a play; often including the actors and other visual elements of each setting or of changes within a setting. A storyboard is an elementary, visual, linear account – a kind of comic strip showing what a production might or will look like.

Theatre: A cultural form that continues to reinvent and rediscover itself despite the invention of film, television and other media. From ceremonial ritual to entertainment, theatre in its many forms is a celebration of the communal experience people can have with one another in real time. Increasingly you may encounter electronic elements as well as live performers on stage but the audience will usually be enjoying a collective, live experience. As it has been associated with social and political commentary, or

because it is regarded as escapist entertainment, it is a form that it is convenient for many to overlook and to marginalise. Reports of its demise are premature. Theatre is sometimes used as a shorthand to cover all kinds of performance, from opera to ballet to puppetry and all kinds of buildings dedicated for performance from a small studio theatre to an opera house.

Thrust Stage: A stage that extends forward, beyond the proscenium, into the audience. It is sometimes felt to offer a closer and more 'authentic' engagement with the audience than action behind the proscenium arch. This was a 20th-century replacement of the old forestage. See also Scenic Stage.

Trompe l'oeil: A French term used to describe optical effects pioneered by painters during the Renaissance and designed to deceive the viewer's eye into believing that it is looking at three rather than two dimensions. See also Renaissance and Perspective.

Tulle: A delicate, thin, silk network fabric.

Unit Sets: One of the expressions used for a single setting that is versatile enough for all of the changes required in a play. Several of the designers in this book talk about creating single settings that can synchronise all of the elements of a production, as opposed to creating a fresh setting for each act or scene.

Wings: The space available, out of the audience's eye, on either side of the stage. Older theatres tend to be relatively small and often have tiny wing spaces. Coincidentally these are often the theatres that present the big musicals. This creates quite a challenge for the company (or the ensemble) and an even greater challenge for the stage designer who has to find a way of hanging and storing flats and other stage apparatus. Some modern opera houses and theatres that run shows in repertory have additional storage above and to the side of the stage so that an entire set can be flown and stored.

Visual material contributed by Günther Schneider-Siemssen: p14 **Ring Cycle**, with thanks and acknowledgement to Metropolitan Opera, New York; p17 (1–3) **Un Re in Ascolto**, with thanks and acknowledgement to the Salzburg Festspielhaus, Salzburg; pp18–19 (1–7) **De Temporum Fine Comedia**, with thanks and acknowledgement to the Salzburg Festspielhaus, Salzburg; pp20–21 (1–6) **Tales of Hoffmann**, with thanks and acknowledgement to the Salzburg Marionettentheater, Salzburg; pp22–25 (1–6) **Ring Cycle**, with thanks and acknowledgement to Metropolitan Opera, New York; p24 (1–2) **Ring Cycle**, with thanks and acknowledgement to the Royal Opera House, London; p25 (1–2) **Ring Cycle**, with thanks and acknowledgement to the Wagner Festival, Wels

Visual material contributed by Ralph Koltai: pp26–29 (1–6) **Taverner**, with thanks and acknowledgement to the Royal Opera House, London; pp30–31 (1–4) **The Planets**, with thanks and acknowledgement to the Royal Opera House, London; pp32–34 (1–3) **Die Soldaten**, with thanks and acknowledgement to Lyons Opera, Lyons; p34 (1–4) **Baal**, with thanks and acknowledgement to the Royal Shakespeare Company, Stratford; p36 (3–5) **Metropolis**, with thanks and acknowledgement to the Piccadilly Theatre, London

Visual material contributed by Ming Cho Lee: p38 (1) **The Hollow Lands**, with thanks and acknowledgement to the South West Repertory Theatre, Costa Mesa; p41 (1–6) **Khovanshchina**, with thanks and acknowledgement to the Metropolitan Opera, New York; pp42–43 (1, 4–5) **Macbeth**, with thanks and acknowledgement to the Shakespeare Theatre, Washington D.C.; pp44–45 (1–9) **The Hollow Lands**, with thanks and acknowledgement to South West Repertory Theatre, Costa Mesa; p48 (1–2) **Rashomon**, with thanks and acknowledgement to Grazer Opernhaus, Graz; p49 (1) **Electra**, with thanks and acknowledgement to New York Shakespeare Festival Delacorte Theater, New York

Visual material contributed by Guy-Claude François: p50 **Terre Etrangère**, with thanks and acknowledgement to the National Theatre of Finland, Helsinki; p52 (1–3) **L'Indiade**, with thanks and acknowledgement to Théâtre de Soleil, Paris; p53 (1–3) **L'Age d'Or**, with thanks and acknowledgement to Théâtre de Soleil, Paris; pp54–55 (1–2) **Les Atrides**, with thanks and acknowledgement to Théâtre de Soleil, Paris; p55 (1–4) **La Ville Parjure**, with thanks and acknowledgement to Théâtre de Soleil, Paris; p56 (1–2) **Macbeth**, with thanks and acknowledgement to Opéra de Nancy, Nancy; p57 (1–2) **Richard II**, with thanks and acknowledgement to Théâtre de Soleil, Paris; p57 (3–4) **A Midsummer Night's Dream**, with thanks and acknowledgement to Théâtre de Soleil, Paris; p58 (1) **Life is a Dream**, with thanks and acknowledgement to Théâtre de Vasteras, Stockholm; p58 (1) **The Miser**, with thanks and acknowledgement to Théâtre de Vasteras, Stockholm; p59 (1) **The Misanthrope**, with thanks and acknowledgement to Atelier Théâtral, Brussels; p59 (1–2) **Terre Etrangère**, with thanks and acknowledgement to the National Theatre of Finland, Helsinki; p60 (1–2) **Mephisto**, with thanks and acknowldegement to Théâtre de Soleil, Paris; p61 (1) *Molière*, with thanks and acknowldegement to Ariane Mnouchkine and (2) *Jefferson in Paris*, with thanks and acknowldegement to Merchant Ivory Pictures

Visual material contributed by Jaroslav Malina: p62 (1) *Way to Paradise*; pp64–65 (1–5) **Leon and Lena**, with thanks and acknowledgement to Drama Studio, Usti nad labem; pp66–67 (1–6) **Don Juan**, with thanks and acknowledgement to Municipal Theatre, Zlin; pp68–69 (1–4) **Zajíc, Zajíc**, with thanks and acknowledgement to the Municipal Theatre, Zlin; pp70–73 (1–7), **The Insect Play**, with thanks and acknowledgement to the National Theatre, Prague; pp74–75 (1–7) **A Magpie in the Hand**, with thanks and acknowledgement to Juraj Herz

Visual material contributed by Bill Dudley: p76 **Lucia di Lammermoor**, with thanks and acknowledgement to Bastille Opera, Paris; pp78–79 (2–4) **The Homecoming**, with thanks and acknowledgement to the Royal National Theatre, London (2–4); pp80–81 (1–5) **Lucia di Lammermoor**, with thanks and acknowledgement to Bastille Opera, Paris; pp82–84 (1–5) **The Big Picnic**, with thanks and acknowledgement to Promenade Productions; pp84–85 (1–4) **The Ship**, with thanks and acknowledgement to Promenade Productions; pp86–87 (1–5) **Maria Stuart**, with thanks and acknowledgement to the Royal National Theatre, London; p88 (1–5) **The Dance of the Vampires**, with thanks and acknowledgement to the Vienna State Opera, Vienna; p89 (3) **Cleo, Camping, Emmanuelle and Dick**, with thanks and acknowledgement to the Royal National Theatre, London

Visual material contributed by Maria Björnson: p90 **Macbeth**, with thanks and acknowledgement to Teatro alla Scala, Milan; p94 (1, 3, 5, 7) **Macbeth**, with thanks and acknowledgement to Teatro alla Scala, Milan; pp96–97 (1–11) **The Marriage of Figaro**, with thanks and acknowledgement to The Grand Theatre, Geneva; pp98–99 (1–7) **The Cunning Little Vixen**, with thanks and acknowledgement to the Welsh National Opera, Cardiff; pp100–101 (1–3, 5) **The Phantom of the Opera**, with thanks and acknowledgement to Her Majesty's Theatre, London

Visual material contributed by JC Serroni: p102 **Zero**, with thanks and acknowledgement to Teatro Municipal, São Paulo; pp104–105 (1–3) **New Old Story**, with thanks and acknowledgement to Teatro Anchieta, São Paulo; p107 (1–5) **Salvation Path**, with thanks and acknowledgement to Teatro Anchieta, São Paulo; pp108–111 (1–6) **Dracula and other Vampires**, with thanks and acknowledgement to Teatro Anchieta, São Paulo; p112 (1–2) **North Side Paradise**, with thanks and acknowledgement to Teatro Anchieta, São Paulo; p113 (1–3) **The Coffee Trade Foxes**, with thanks and acknowledgement to Teatro Aliança Francesa, São Paulo

Visual material contributed by Yukio Horio: p114 **Buddha**, with thanks and acknowledgement to New National Theatre, Tokyo; pp116–117 (1–3) **2/2**, with thanks and acknowledgement to Bunkamura Theatre, Tokyo; pp118–119 (1–5) **Romeo and Juliet**, with thanks and acknowledgement to Saitama Arts Theatre, Tokyo; pp120–121 (1–7) **Richard III**, with thanks and acknowledgement to Saitama Arts Theatre, Tokyo; pp122–123 (1–6) **Buddha**, with thanks and acknowledgement to New National Theatre, Tokyo; pp124–125 (1–4) **Kiru**, with thanks and acknowledgement to Osaka Kintetsu Theatre, Osaka

Visual material contributed by Richard Hudson: pp126–129 **Oklahoma!**, with thanks and acknowledgement to UK Tour, 1994; pp130–131 (1–4) **Guillaume Tell**, with thanks and acknowledgement to Vienna State Opera, Vienna; pp132–133 (1–7, 9) **Samson et Dalila**, with thanks and acknowledgement to Metropolitan Opera, New York; pp134–135 (1–4) **Lucia di Lammermoor**, with thanks and acknowledgement to Zurich Opera, Zurich; pp136–137 (1–4) **The Lion King** ©1997 Disney Enterprises, Inc.; pp138–139 (1–12) **Into the Woods**, with thanks and acknowledgement to the Phoenix Theatre, London

Visual material contributed by Adrianne Lobel: p140 **Nixon in China**, with thanks and acknowledgement to Houston Grand Opera, Houston; p143 (2–6) **Lady in the Dark**, with thanks and acknowledgement to the Royal National Theatre, London; pp144–145 (2–11) **L'Allegro, il Penseroso ed il Moderato**, with thanks and acknowledgement to Théâtre de la Monnaie, Brussels; pp146–147 (1–4, 6–9) **The Marriage of Figaro**, with thanks and acknowledgement to Pepsico Summerfare, New York; p148 (1–3) **The Diary of Anne Frank**, with thanks and acknowledgement to Music Box Theatre, New York; p149 (1–3) **On the Town**, with thanks and acknowledgement to New York Shakespeare Festival Delacorte Theatre, New York; p150 (1–9) **Nixon in China**, with thanks and acknowledgement to Houston Grand Opera; p152–153 (1–7) **Platée**, with thanks and acknowledgement to the Royal Opera House, London

Visual material contributed by George Tsypin: p154 **War and Peace**, with thanks and acknowledgement to the Kirov Opera of St Petersburg and the Metropolitan Opera, New York; pp156–157 (1–4) **Ring Cycle: The Rhinegold**, with thanks and acknowledgement to Netherlands Opera, Amsterdam; p158 (1–4) **Ring Cycle: The Valkyrie**, with thanks and acknowledgement to Netherlands Opera, Amsterdam; p159 (1–3) **Ring Cycle: Siegfried**, with thanks and acknowledgement to Netherlands Opera, Amsterdam; p159 (1) **Ring Cycle: The Twilight of the Gods**, with thanks and acknowledgement to Netherlands Opera, Amsterdam; pp160–161 (1–8) **Saint Francis of Assisi**, with thanks and acknowledgement to the Salzburg Festival, Salzburg and the Bastille Opera, Paris; pp162–163 (1–6) **War and Peace**, with thanks and acknowledgement to the Kirov Opera of St Petersburg and the Metropolitan Opera, New York; pp164–165 (1–3) **Oedipus Rex**, with thanks and acknowledgement to the Saito Kine Festival, Matsamoto

Special acknowledgements: p42 (2) **Macbeth**, photography by Carol Pratt; p43 (3) **Macbeth**, photography by Carol Rosegg; p46–47 (10) **The Hollow Lands**, photography by Ken Howard; p48 (1) **Rashomon**, with thanks and acknowledgement to the Opernhaus Graz; p48 (3) **Rashomon**, photography by Winnie Klotz; p65 (2) **Leon and Lena**, photography by Karel Honsa; p66 (2–3) **Don Juan**, photography by Dusan Simanek; p67 (5–6) **Don Juan**, photography by Bohdan Holomicek; p68 (2–3) **Zajíc, Zajíc**, photography by Jan Regel; p72 (3–4) **The Insect Play**, photography by Dusan Simanek; p74 (4–6) **A Magpie in the Hand**, photography by Jiri Kucera; p93 (3) **Katya Kabanova** © Catherine Ashmore; p90, 94 (2, 4, 6, 8) **Macbeth**, photography by Andrea Tamoni, with thanks and acknowledgement to Teatro alla Scala, Milan; p93 (4) **Katya Kabanova** © Clive Barda; p101 (4) **The Phantom of the Opera** © Clive Barda; p114 **Buddha**, photography by Kaori Mashuhira; p116–117 (1–3) **2/2**, photography by Kaori Mashuhira; p119 (3–5) **Romeo and Juliet**, photography by Izumi Murakami; pp120–121 (1–3, 6–7) **Richard III**, photography by Izumi Murakami; p122 (1–6) **Buddha**, photography by Kaori Mashuhira; pp124–125 (1–4) **Kiru**, photography by Kaori Mashuhira; p138 (7) **Into the Woods**, photography by Michael Le Trench; p148 (1) **The Diary of Anne Frank**, photography by Carol Rosegg; p149 (3) **On the Town**, photography by Michael Daniels

Courtesy The Bridgeman Art Library: *Proportions of the Human Figure* (*Vitruvian Man*), c1492, by Leonardo da Vinci; p78 (1) *Study for Crouching Nude, 1952*, by Francis Bacon, The Detroit Institute of Arts, Detroit, USA © Estate of Francis Bacon/ARS, NY and DACS, London 2000; p80 (6) *Jeantaud, Linet and Laine*, 1871, by Edgar Dégas, Musee d'Orsay, Paris, Giraudon/Bridgeman Art Library, London: p134 (8) *Ballantine* 1948–60, by Franz Kline, Los Angeles County Museum of Art, CA, USA/Bridgeman Art Library © ARS, NY and DACS; p142 (1) *Sailboats*, 1929, by Lyonel Feininger, The Detroit Institute of Arts, USA/ © DACS; p144 (1) *Homage to the Square: Joy*, 1964, by Josef Albers, James Goodman Gallery, New York © DACS 2000; p144 (2) *Untitled*, 1951–55, by Mark Rothko, Tate Gallery, London © Kate Rothko Prizel and Christopher Rothko/DACS 2000; p146 (5) *La Fête à Saint-Cloud*, by Jean-Honore Fragonard, Banque de France, Paris/Pete Willis/Bridgeman Art Library

Courtesy Kobal Picture Archive: p36 (1) *Modern Times*; (2) *Metropolis*, with thanks and acknowledgement to the National Film Archive

Courtesy The National Gallery, London: p86 (2) *Landscape with Psyche Outside the Palace of Cupid*, 1664, Claude Lorraine © National Gallery, London

Courtesy Georgina Masters: p89 (1) *The Villages of England*, 1932, and (2) *The Spirit of London*, 1937, both by Brian Cook © Estate Brian Cook, Batsford

Courtesy The Munch Museum, Oslo: p92 (1) *Despair*, 1893, by Munch © Munch Museum/Munch – Ellingsen Group, BONO, Oslo, DACS, London 2000

Courtesy The National Gallery of Art, Washington D.C.: p92 (2) *Puddles*, 1952, by M.C. Escher © 2000 Cordon Art B. V., Baarn, Holland

Courtesy Dover Pictorial Archive: p97 (6–7) *28* and *29 from Perspective*, Jan Vredeman de Vries © 1968 Dover Publications

Although every effort has been made to contact owners of material reproduced in this book we have not always been successful. In the event of a copyright query, please contact the publishers.